# THE NEW GOOD CAKE BOOK

G·K
Hall
&Cº

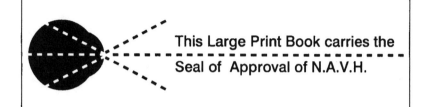

This Large Print Book carries the
Seal of Approval of N.A.V.H.

# THE NEW
# GOOD CAKE
# BOOK

## Over 125 delicious
## recipes that can
## be prepared in
## 30 minutes or less

# DIANA DALSASS

**G.K. Hall & Co.**
**Thorndike, Maine**

Published in 1997 by arrangement with W.W. Norton & Co., Inc.

G.K. Hall Large Print Reference Collection.

The text of this Large Print edition is unabridged.
Other aspects of the book may vary from the original edition.

Set in 16 pt. Plantin by Juanita Macdonald.

Printed in the United States on permanent paper.

**Library of Congress Cataloging in Publication Data**

Dalsass, Diana.
    The new good cake book : over 125 delicious recipes
    that can be prepared in 30 minutes or less / Diana Dalsass.
        p.    cm.
    Reprint. Originally published : W.W. Norton. 1982.
    Includes index.
    ISBN 0-7838-8050-2 (lg. print : hc : alk. paper)
    1. Cake.   2. Quick and easy cookery.   I. Title.
TX771.D35   1997
    641.8´653—dc21                                    96-48726

This book is dedicated
to my daughter,
# ADRIA,
who is always
an enthusiastic critic
and taster of all my cakes.

# CONTENTS

# Chapter One

# Chapter Two

# Chapter Three

# Chapter Four

# Chapter Five

# Chapter Six

# Chapter Seven

# Chapter Eight

# Chapter Nine

## Special-Occasion Cakes

# Chapter Ten

## Bonus Cake Recipes

# Chapter Eleven

# INTRODUCTION

More than a decade ago, the original *Good Cake Book* was published. The premise of the book was simple. Although I had encountered many cookbooks, there were few devoted solely to cakes. And the handful that was generally focused on layer cakes that were spread with a variety of ultrarich fillings. Sometimes, it seemed that the fillings and frosting took precedence over the cake itself.

My cakes, on the other hand, could stand unadorned. Rather than being fluffy little layers, these cakes contained fruits, nuts, chocolate, and other delectable embellishments. Beyond the enhancements to the batter itself, some cakes were marbleized, others contained a baked-on topping that added new dimensions of flavor and texture, while yet others were layered with a spicy streusel filling.

Furthermore, the cakes were remarkably easy to put together. Since all the recipes followed one of two basic methods of assembly, once the home baker mastered the technique for just one cake, dozens of others could be whipped up using the same technique. Perhaps most important for today, when no one has extra time to spare, the batter for all of these cakes could be made in 30 minutes or less.

The response to *The Good Cake Book* was overwhelmingly positive. (There's something about a wholesome gingerbread or homey banana loaf or never-fail chocolate cake that makes cooks everywhere feel good about baking.) The recipes not only *sounded* easy to make and foolproof; they, in fact, *were.*

No one, since the publication of *The Good Cake Book*, has ever complained of a cake recipe of mine that doesn't work. Instead, people who try my recipes brag that their cakes are even better when *they* make them because they add more raisins or substitute pecans for walnuts or stud the batter with blueberries — all good and tasty ideas.

A glance at the dedication in *The Good Cake Book* ("To my husband, Mario, . . . who could not get through the day without at least one piece of homemade cake") gives readers an idea of just how many cakes I bake — at least one each weekend, in fact. Not only do my husband and I eat cake, we've been joined by a daughter who will consider no other dessert beyond cake and ice cream. This translates into a lot of new cake recipes tested over the past decade.

The best of the recipes have been culled into this volume, *The New Good Cake Book* — 133 easily assembled cakes to bake, to savor, to enjoy, to share. I am so certain that each of these cake recipes will bake up flawlessly that I invite any user of this book who experiences a problem with a recipe to write to me care of W. W. Norton & Company, Inc., 500 Fifth Avenue, New York, NY 10110-0017; I will personally answer any question.

# The Basics of Cake Baking

One reason why cake baking is so quick and easy (and nearly foolproof) is that there are only two basic methods for combining the ingredients. Once you've mastered these, virtually every cake recipe you'll encounter will be a snap.

## METHOD FOR BUTTER CAKES

The most common type of cake is the butter cake. The procedure for making this kind of cake is always the same; all that varies is the choice of flavorings for the cake. Here are the steps involved:

1. The butter (or margarine) is first creamed with the sugar (or molasses, honey, maple syrup, and so forth). For best results, the butter should be soft, but not melting or oily, before beginning. Beat the sugar into the butter until the butter is very light and fluffy. While you can use a spoon for this step, an electric mixer does the job quicker and easier. (In the following section, I discuss how to prepare cake batters using a food processor.)
2. Next, the eggs are beaten into the butter-sugar mixture. These should also be beaten very well, until the mixture looks completely uniform. Many recipes instruct the cook to beat in the eggs one at a time, but this is unnecessary as long as the eggs are thoroughly incorporated before you proceed to the next step.

3. Now the liquid ingredients and flavorings — such as milk, juice, melted chocolate, applesauce, vanilla extract, pumpkin puree, and so forth — are beaten into the batter. The consistency will be liquidy, and the batter may even look curdled. Don't worry about it. Some recipes instruct the baker to add the liquid ingredients alternately with the dry ones; this is time-consuming, bothersome, and unnecessary.

4. The dry ingredients — flour, leavening, salt, and spice — are now stirred together in a separate bowl. With today's light flours, it is not necessary to sift the dry ingredients or to sift the flour before measuring it, which would mean extra utensils for you to wash and would add to the preparation time.

5. The dry ingredients are then beaten or stirred into the liquid ones. I usually use a large mixing spoon for this, but you can also use an electric mixer on low speed. Do not overbeat the dry ingredients; mix just until the flour is fully incorporated into the mixture.

6. Occasionally, a recipe will call for the egg whites to be beaten separately (although few recipes in this book subject the baker to this extra — and usually unnecessary — step). For those few recipes that require the added lightness of beaten egg whites, the whites are folded in gently but thoroughly at this point.

7. Finally, any hard ingredients such as fresh or dried fruits, nuts, or chocolate chips are stirred

into the batter.

8. As the last step, the batter is turned into a greased and floured pan and baked in a pre-heated oven. Be certain that your oven gauge is accurate. Although you may not notice your oven being off by 25°F or so when baking vegetables or casseroles, a small temperature variation — especially an upward one — can have an adverse effect on cakes.

A cake is done when a toothpick inserted in the center of the cake comes out clean, the edges of the cake have pulled away slightly from the sides of the pan, and the cake feels springy when you touch it. Since all ovens are different, begin testing the cake for doneness about 10 minutes before the time specified in the recipe. Let the cake cool on a rack, and don't remove it from the pan until it has reached room temperature.

## FOOD-PROCESSOR METHOD FOR BUTTER CAKES

If you own a food processor, the steps for making butter cakes with it are identical to those described above, only speeded up enormously. Here are some tips:

• Always use the steel blade.
• If the cake is small (such as an 8" or 9" square), the entire batter can be prepared in the food processor's work bowl. If the cake is larger (for example, a layer cake, tube cake, or large rec-

tangular cake), process everything except the dry ingredients in the work bowl. Then, by hand, stir the contents of the work bowl into the dry ingredients, which have been placed in a large mixing bowl.

- If the recipe calls for lemon or orange rind, you need not grate it separately. Simply peel off the zest (colored portion of the rind) with a vegetable peeler, and add it to the work bowl in step 1 with the butter and sugar. By the time the sugar has been incorporated into the butter, the zest will be finely shredded.
- Ingredients to be chopped, such as nuts, cranberries, apples, chocolate, and so forth, can either be processed before you start making the batter, removed from the work bowl, and stirred into the batter after the dry ingredients have been added, or added to the work bowl after the liquid ingredients have been processed until smooth.

## METHOD FOR OIL (OR MELTED BUTTER) CAKES

Tortes, brownies, chiffon cakes, and carrot cakes are among those that most commonly fit into this category. The procedure for making oil-based cakes is similar to that described for butter cakes. It is only in the first two steps that the directions differ:

1. Beat the eggs quite well (with an electric mixer or food processor). Then add the sugar very

gradually, beating all the while. When finished, the mixture should be thick and pale yellow in color. It is this thorough beating that gives these kinds of cake the appropriate texture — chewy as in brownies, spongelike for chiffon cakes, and so forth.

2. Beat the oil or the slightly cooled, melted butter or margarine into the egg mixture. From this point on, follow the procedure for butter cakes.

# Notes on Common Cake Ingredients

## BUTTER VERSUS MARGARINE

Butter has an unquestionably finer, fresher flavor than margarine. But butter is also more expensive and high in cholesterol and saturated fats, which can contribute to heart disease and other disorders.

However, from a health standpoint, margarine is not ideal either. When the polyunsaturated liquid oils that go into margarine are processed to make them solid, their chemical composition changes, and the resulting fat may be as bad as — or even worse than — butter. In general, softer margarines are nutritionally healthier, but these usually do not work well in baked goods.

In most recipes, I specify butter or margarine and leave the choice to you. But when the flavor of butter is essential, I state this, and you really should try to use at least half butter.

Some cakes call for a liquid shortening, usually unflavored vegetable or salad oil. I have found, however, that oil can produce an unpleasant, slightly greasy texture. In recipes of this type, I usually prefer to substitute melted butter or margarine, which results in a better cake.

## LIQUIDS

The most common liquid used in cake batters is milk or a milk product such as yogurt or sour cream.

When milk is specified in a recipe, you may use whole, low-fat, skim, or reconstituted nonfat dry milk. The slightly different fat content of each will not affect the final result.

When "sour" milk or buttermilk is specified, you may make your own substitute from ordinary milk. For each cup called for, place 1 tablespoon of vinegar or lemon juice in the bottom of the measuring cup. Fill the cup to the 1-cup mark with milk, and stir. You may also use plain yogurt as a substitute. Do *not* use milk that has gone bad or sour in the refrigerator.

When yogurt is specified, you may substitute buttermilk or "sour" milk, made as directed above.

When sour cream is specified, remember that there is nothing else that can duplicate the marvelous texture and flavor that this ingredient lends to a cake. But if you must make the cake immediately and you have no sour cream, you can substitute yogurt, buttermilk, or "sour" milk and add an extra tablespoon of butter or margarine for each cup of sour cream called for.

Other liquids commonly used in cake batter include water, coffee, alcohol, fruit juices, and fruit purees. Occasionally, a recipe will call for heavy or whipping cream in place of both the butter and the liquid. In this instance, it is best not to use a substitute for the heavy cream.

## FLOUR

Whenever I specify flour in this book, I am referring to all-purpose white flour, either bleached or unbleached, as you prefer. It is not necessary to use cake flour in these recipes.

Whole-wheat flour is also called for in several recipes throughout the book. This type of flour, which includes the germ and bran along with the starchy grain, is heartier and more flavorful than white flour — and more nutritious. Whole-wheat flour is particularly appealing in such cakes as carrot, spice, and banana. Because whole-wheat flour is heavier than white, I usually use half whole wheat and half white to achieve the advantages of both. If you don't have whole-wheat flour on hand (or if you prefer a cake with a less hearty texture), you can use all-purpose flour instead.

## LEAVENING

The two most common leavening (or rising)

agents used in cake baking are baking powder and baking soda. Baking powder is a general, all-purpose leavening agent, and you'll find it in most cake recipes.

Baking soda is usually called for when the cake contains an acidic ingredient — "sour" milk, yogurt — or honey. In these instances, the baking soda chemically reacts with the ingredient, which leads to an especially light and airy cake. But baking soda also has a bitter flavor; if too much is used, its taste will be detected in the cake. This is why my recipes never call for more than 1 teaspoon in a cake. Also, baking soda tends to become lumpy in the box. So, as you're adding it to the bowl with the dry ingredients, be sure to return the baking soda to its powdery form by pressing out any lumps with the back of a spoon.

## ROLLED OATS

Rolled oats are available in three forms: old-fashioned, quick-cooking, and instant. Old-fashioned and quick-cooking are the same except that the groat in quick-cooking oats has been cut into several pieces before being rolled. Either old-fashioned or quick-cooking oats may be used in the recipes in this book. (Instant oats are too highly processed to produce the characteristic chewy oatmeal texture.)

*Note:* All rolled-oat measurements in this book are for *raw* rolled oats measured directly from the package.

# CHOCOLATE

When chocolate flavors the entire cake (rather than bits of chocolate scattered throughout the batter), unsweetened chocolate is generally used. This may be in the form of chocolate squares or cocoa. Both produce similar results when the proper conversion for fat content is followed.

If a recipe calls for unsweetened chocolate and you only have cocoa in the kitchen, you may substitute 3 tablespoons of unsweetened cocoa powder plus 1 tablespoon of butter for each ounce of chocolate. (Do not use cocoa mixes that contain milk and/or sugar.) Likewise, if a recipe specifies cocoa, you may use a 1-ounce square of unsweetened chocolate for every 3 tablespoons of cocoa; for each square of chocolate used, cut back on the butter called for in the recipe by 1 table-spoon.

There are two types of unsweetened cocoa powder generally available, alkalized and nonalkalized, which refer to the method of processing the cocoa beans. Hershey's Cocoa, found in most supermarkets, is alkalized. Nonalkalized cocoa, of which Droste's is the best-known example, is also referred to as "Dutch process" cocoa. This cocoa is usually more difficult to find and is also generally more expensive.

The type of cocoa you choose to use depends on your taste preferences since both types work well in the recipes in this book. I prefer alkalized cocoa because I find the flavor to be more intensely chocolate. Nonalkalized cocoa is darker in color, but the chocolate flavor is milder.

While bakers use unsweetened chocolate or cocoa to flavor the cake batter itself, for chunks of chocolate, we turn to semisweet chips or morsels. To my way of thinking, dark chocolate is so delicious, almost any brand will suffice for all baking needs.

But recently, a new dark chocolate came to my attention. A food editor at the *New York Times* devoted nearly a full page to describing the superior quality of Hawaiian Vintage Chocolate, praising it as being superior to even the finest Belgian chocolate. Intrigued, I had to sample it. Since this chocolate is only sold wholesale, the minimum order was 8 pounds, which came in the form of disks, each about four times bigger than ordinary chocolate chips.

This is the best chocolate I have ever tasted, and nothing else will now suffice for me or my family. Even my daughter insists on baking with it. Hawaiian Vintage Chocolate is richer and more intensely flavored than any other chocolate I have sampled. And since the taste lingers in your mouth, a small amount is immensely satisfying — as though you've eaten a great deal more of it than you actually have. (Because these chocolate pieces are larger than chocolate chips, you will need to chop them before adding them to your cake batter.)

Hawaiian Vintage Chocolate is available by mail directly from the distributor, Continental

Foods in Olathe, Kansas. Call 1-800-345-1543 for ordering information.

*A note on melting chocolate:* Because chocolate melts at a low temperature, it's easy to scorch it if you're not careful. Many cookbooks suggest melting chocolate in a double boiler. Although this eliminates the risk of burning, it does take longer. If, however, you use a very low heat, stir the chocolate occasionally, and remove the pot from the heat as soon as the chocolate has melted, this precaution isn't necessary.

## SPICES

For certain spices such as nutmeg, some cooks prefer to grind them just before using. Personally, I find the fragrance of bottled spices sufficiently heady and do not see an advantage in taking the extra step of grinding the spices myself. However, if you prefer freshly ground spices, by all means substitute them whenever you wish. Since most people do rely on the spices available in jars, it's important to note that these are best used within a year of purchase. Kept longer than that, their flavor diminishes.

Whenever spices are called for in this book, I mean the ground version (for example, ground cinnamon or ground nutmeg, or ground ginger). The only time I *specify* the ground version in a recipe is when cloves are used. This is because some recipes (in other cookbooks) do call for whole cloves, such as when studding a ham. Also, whole cloves are so small, a reader might think that ¼ teaspoon of cloves, for example, refers to the number of whole cloves that would fit into this measure. So, to avoid any possible confusion, I list this ingredient as "ground cloves."

## VANILLA

In the recipes in this book that call for vanilla, I refer to pure vanilla extract. Imitation extract has an unappealing flavor and shouldn't be used.

Just as some cooks prefer to use freshly ground spices, some like to use the vanilla bean rather than the extract. My own view is that this is tedious and unnecessary except when making the most delicate of vanilla-flavored desserts such as homemade vanilla ice cream.

If you choose to use the bean, steep it in hot liquid for about 20 minutes, then grind it in a food processor, reserving the liquid for the recipe as well. (Thus, if the recipe calls for milk, heat the milk and steep the vanilla bean in it. Cool the milk before adding it to the recipe.)

Another alternative is to make vanilla sugar. Place a vanilla bean in a jar containing about 2 cups of sugar. After a week or so, the sugar in the jar will have a subtle vanilla flavor.

# Improvisation

Some people believe that baking requires such exact measuring that there's no room for individual expression. While it is true that the proportion of dry to liquid ingredients should not be altered except by experienced bakers, there are ways that any home baker can add his or her own touches to cakes.

For example, one dried fruit can easily be substituted for another. As you'll note if you look through these recipes, I am partial to raisins. But if you prefer chopped dates, dried apricots, dried figs, or other dried fruits, use them instead.

Similarly, I like walnuts. But others may favor pecans, almonds, or macadamia nuts. Again, it's easy to switch from one to the other.

If a cake calls for chocolate chips and you're cutting back on fats or are allergic to chocolate, feel free to substitute dried fruits or to omit the ingredient altogether. (This applies only when whole chocolate chips are added to the batter, not when they are melted and become an ingredient in the cake batter itself.)

Liquids, too, can be varied. If a recipe calls for water, you can add more flavor by substituting coffee or fruit juice. But do not make this substitution for milk since it will alter the texture of the cake.

When interchanging fresh fruits, try to substitute types similar to what was called for in the recipe — for example, pears for apples, raspberries for blueberries, plums for peaches.

The fact is, if you start with a good basic cake recipe, a few minor changes should not turn it into a disaster. And if all substitutions work well, the final result may be more to your liking than the original.

# Some General Notes on Baking

## MEASURING CUPS

Considerable time can be saved by using the graduated dry measuring cups that come in $1/4$-, $1/3$-, $1/2$-, and 1-cup sizes. For measuring flour, sugar, or other dry ingredients, all you need do is scoop the cup into the bag or canister, fill it to overflowing, and then level off the top with a knife. It takes about 5 seconds to measure a cup of flour this way — far less time than if filling a glass measuring cup a spoonful at a time.

Although you can use dry measuring cups for liquids, it's probably easier to use the glass ones so that the liquid doesn't spill over when the cup is filled to the top.

## PREPARATION OF BAKING PANS FOR EASY REMOVAL OF CAKES

It's easy to remove cakes from their baking pans if you follow these two simple steps.

First, grease and flour the pan by smearing all inside surfaces with margarine or shortening, or spray the pan with a liquid oil like Pam. Sprinkle about a tablespoon of flour into the pan, and tilt the pan to spread the flour evenly over all the surfaces. Standing over the kitchen sink, turn the pan upside down, and tap it against the side of the sink a few times to get rid of any excess flour.

Second, to make sure the baked cake doesn't stick to the sides of the pan, when the cake comes out of the oven, immediately run a knife around the edges of the pan. After the cake has cooled to room temperature, again run a knife around the edges of the pan, this time pulling up gently on the bottom of the cake to dislodge it from the pan. After you have gone around the pan in this fashion, simply tip the cake upside down over a plate, and it will slide out. The cake is now upside down.

If the cake has a firm texture, you can pick it up and reinvert it so that it is right side up. If the cake is delicate or if you are concerned about it breaking in your hands, put another plate on top of the upside-down cake. Turn the cake over, and remove the plate that is now on top.

If you are baking a tube cake, you will find that it is easier to remove the cake from the pan if the pan is a two-piece one, in which the central cone is attached to the bottom of the pan and is separate from the outer rim.

Whether you choose a one-piece or two-piece tube pan, follow the instructions above to remove the cake. Because the tube cake is much thicker than a flat cake, it is especially important to run the knife around the edges and central core of the pan to loosen the cake before tipping it out of the pan.

There are two basic types of tube pan. One has a flat bottom like other cake pans. The top crust comes out crisp and attractive; therefore the cake should be reinverted after being tipped out of the pan so that the top crust remains on top.

The other type of pan is a Bundt pan and has a fluted bottom and sides. When cakes are baked in a Bundt pan, they are kept upside down for serving so that the decorative part of the cake is on top. These cakes are particularly attractive when drizzled with a glaze or icing.

The recipes in this book that specify using a tube pan may be baked in either a flat-bottom tube pan or a fluted Bundt pan.

## BAKING-PAN SIZES

If you bake cakes often, you probably own baking pans of different sizes and shapes. But even if your kitchen is equipped with only a few pans, many sizes are interchangeable. For flat cakes (those baked in square, round, or oblong pans), just compute the number of square inches in the pan specified in the recipe, and then use the pan you own with the closest size to this. If the cake is a little flatter or higher, the final result will still be fine. Just add or subtract a few minutes from the baking time to compensate for the difference in thickness.

For example, if a recipe specifies a 9" X 9" square baking pan (81 square inches), you can substitute an 8" X 10" oblong pan (80 square inches). The baking time may be increased by about 5 minutes. Likewise, if a recipe specifies a 9" X 13" oblong pan (117 square inches), you could substitute two 9" round layer cake pans (61 square inches each = 122 square inches total). In this instance, the baking time may be a little shorter.

When a tube pan is called for, you may use a 9" or 10" flat-bottom tube pan or a fluted Bundt pan of similar size. Or the cake may be baked in two 9" X 5" loaf pans. If you use loaf pans, begin testing the cakes for doneness about 10 minutes before the time given in the recipe.

*Note:* A cake made from a recipe that specifies a tube or loaf pan may or may not bake properly in a flat pan (and vice versa). If you wish to convert from one pan to the other, try it out and hope for the best. (See the Appendix "Comparative Baking-Pan Sizes," page 348.)

## NUMBER OF SERVINGS

For each recipe in the book, I have estimated the number of servings you can expect to get from the cake. In doing so, I have taken into account the cake's richness as well as its size. For instance, many people would prefer a smaller serving of a buttery cake containing lots of chocolate chips and a larger serving of a plainer cake.

While it might seem to make sense that a 9" X 13" baking pan, for example, would yield the same number of servings each time you baked a cake in it, the fact is that cake recipes vary in terms of how much batter is produced. Thus, I will suggest cutting one cake into smaller squares because it is higher than another cake baked in that same pan.

You should understand that all cake yields listed in this book are estimates. I often find that when I'm slicing a cake for guests, some of them view a skimpy sliver as an appropriate serving while others are not satisfied unless they are given a generously thick slice. So use my suggested number of servings as only a guide, and consider the appetites of those who will be eating your cakes.

## STORAGE OF CAKES

It is much easier to store an unfrosted cake than one with gooey icing that sticks to plastic wrap or one that is cream-filled and readily spoils.

Most of the cakes in this book have only to be protected from drying out. You may cover them with plastic wrap or foil, or place them in one of those glass or plastic cake keepers. Cake stored this way will generally stay fresh for about a week.

Depending on the moistness of the cake and the temperature and humidity of your home, you may wish to refrigerate the cake as well as wrap it. Plainer cakes, such as gingerbread, brownies, and spice cakes, usually fare well at room temperature unless it's a humid summer day. However, cakes that contain fresh fruits can be very moist and should be refrigerated, particularly during the warm months, to protect them against spoilage. If you prefer to eat your cake at room temperature, just remove it from the refrigerator an hour or so before eating it.

For longer storage, a cake — frosted or unfrosted — may be frozen. Thaw the cake at room temperature, keeping it wrapped to prevent it from drying out.

## HIGH-ALTITUDE BAKING

Any place that is over 3,000 feet above sea level is considered high altitude when it comes to baking, and the higher the altitude, the greater the adjustments that need to be made.

The reason why cakes bake differently at higher altitudes is that the air pressure is lower, so the cakes rise more rapidly than at lower elevations. Thus, all high-altitude adjustments are designed to prevent too rapid a rise. Adjustments include lowering the oven temperature, reducing the amount of baking powder or baking soda in a recipe, and reducing the sugar slightly.

The appendix on page 347 provides guidelines for how to adjust the recipes in this book when baking at a high altitude. Please note, though, that some trial and error may be necessary for the texture of the cakes to be ideal, particularly if you

35

are baking them at a very high altitude.

That covers the basics of cake baking. Just a few simple steps, and you have a host of great-tasting, impressive-looking cakes in your repertoire. The only hard part will be deciding which one to make!

The recipes in this book are organized into eleven chapters, with such broad headings as "Chocolate Forever," "Spice Cakes," "Biscotti," "Reduced-Fat Cakes," and "Bar Cakes." Chapter 10 is a bonus: my favorite recipes from the original *Good Cake Book*.

# CHAPTER ONE

# BUTTER CAKES

Cake in its "purest" form is butter cake. A perfect butter cake relies on only the most basic of ingredients — flour, butter, sugar, eggs, vanilla, baking powder and/or baking soda, and salt. (Milk is added for a less dense butter cake, although a true pound cake — the classic butter cake — contains no liquid.) Yet, these few ingredients, when combined in the right proportions and then baked, produce a food that is so basically satisfying almost no one can resist it.

I thought it appropriate that the first chapter of this book take the simple butter cake and add to it a variety of embellishments to bring it to new heights of pleasurable flavor. These recipes call for fresh or dried fruits, spices, nuts, and chocolate. All of these ingredients enhance the butter cake, but none interferes with its smooth, rich quality.

# Red Velvet Cake

I once had occasion to work with a baker who makes cakes for celebrities and sampled his Red Velvet Cake (which he said he always bakes for Lena Horne's birthday). The cake was luscious, but the baker refused to part with the recipe. I was able, however to figure out the "secret ingredient" for myself: browned butter which lends a wonderful nutlike flavor to this pound cake. Although I can't claim that this recipe duplicates his, it's a close enough match for me. If you don't wish to use red food coloring, you may omit it and make Velvet Cake. On the other hand, if you celebrate Saint Patrick's Day, you can easily turn this into a Green Velvet Cake for that holiday.

1½  **sticks (¾ cup) butter or margarine (try to use at least half butter)**
2  **eggs**
2  **cups sugar**
1  **cup milk**
1  **teaspoon vanilla**
1  **teaspoon red food coloring (optional)**
2¾  **cups flour**
1½  **teaspoons baking powder**
¼  **teaspoon salt**

1. Preheat the oven to 350°F.
2. Grease and flour a tube pan.
3. In a large skillet, melt the butter or margarine.

Continue cooking it, swirling the pan occasionally, until it turns light brown at the edges. You don't want to cook it beyond this point, or it will burn. Remove the pan from the heat, and set it aside.

4. In a large bowl, beat the eggs well. Gradually add the sugar, continuing to beat until the mixture is thick and pale yellow. Beat in the browned butter, then the milk, vanilla, and red food coloring (if desired).

5. In another bowl, stir together the flour, baking powder, and salt. Add this to the butter mixture, beating or stirring until the dry ingredients are incorporated.

6. Turn the batter out into the prepared pan. Bake the cake for 1¼ hours or until a toothpick inserted in the highest part of the cake comes out clean. Transfer the pan to a rack to cool.

*Preparation time: 20 minutes*
*Yield: 16 servings*

# Chocolate Chip Pound Cake

Ground almonds and grated orange peel add a subtle flavor to this chocolate chip pound cake. The cake is rich and dense, and slices nicely. Be sure to use mini-chocolate chips or finely chopped regular-size chips. If the chips are too large, they will sink to the bottom of the cake. This is a hearty cake that ships and freezes well.

> 2 sticks (1 cup) butter or margarine, softened (try to use at least half butter)
> 1 cup sugar
> 1 cup brown sugar, preferably dark
> 6 eggs
> ½ cup milk
> 2 teaspoons vanilla
> 1 tablespoon grated orange rind
> 3 cups flour
> 2 teaspoons baking powder
> ¾ cup ground almonds
> 1 cup mini-chocolate chips

1. Preheat the oven to 350°F.
2. Grease and flour a tube pan.
3. In a large bowl, cream the butter or margarine with the sugar and brown sugar until the sugars are fully incorporated. Beat in the eggs, then the milk, vanilla, and orange rind.
4. In another bowl, stir together the flour and

40

baking powder. Add to the creamed mixture, stirring until the dry ingredients are incorporated. Stir in the almonds and chocolate chips.

5. Spread the batter in the prepared pan. Bake the cake for 1 hour 20 minutes or until a toothpick inserted in the highest part of the cake comes out clean. Transfer the pan to a rack to cool.

*Preparation time: 20 minutes*
*Yield: 16 servings*

# Fragrant Butter Cake

Lemon rind and aniseeds lend a delicate flavor to this traditional pound cake, which is especially quick and easy to prepare.

1½ sticks (¾ cup) butter or margarine, softened (try to use at least half butter)
2 cups sugar
3 eggs
Grated rind 1 lemon
¾ cup milk
1 teaspoon vanilla
2¼ cups flour
2 teaspoons baking powder
1½ teaspoons aniseeds
¼ teaspoon salt

1. Preheat the oven to 350°F.
2. Grease and flour a tube pan.
3. In a large bowl, cream the butter or margarine with the sugar until the sugar is fully incorporated. Beat in the eggs, then the lemon rind, milk, and vanilla.
4. In another bowl, stir together the flour, baking powder, aniseeds, and salt. Add to the creamed mixture, stirring until the dry ingredients are incorporated.
5. Turn the batter out into the prepared pan. Bake the cake for 1¼ hours or until a toothpick

inserted in the highest part of the cake comes out clean. Transfer the pan to a rack to cool.

*Preparation time: 20 minutes*
*Yield: 14 to 16 servings*

# Ribbons-of-Fruit Cake

This smooth, buttery pound cake contains a spicy filling of apples and dried tart cherries that lends a lovely flavor and color to each slice. If you can't locate dried tart cherries, substitute dried cranberries. Dried Bing cherries are another option, but decrease the sugar in the filling to 1 tablespoon to compensate for their extra sweetness.

## FILLING
- 3 ounces (½ cup) dried tart cherries
- 1 apple, peeled, cored, and thinly sliced, each slice cut crosswise in half
- 1 teaspoon cinnamon
- 2 teaspoons unsweetened cocoa powder
- ¼ cup sugar

## CAKE
- 2 sticks (1 cup) butter or margarine, softened (try to use at least half butter)
- 1½ cups sugar
- 5 eggs
- 1 teaspoon vanilla
- 1¾ cups flour
- 2 teaspoons baking powder
- ⅛ teaspoon salt

1. To make the filling, in a small bowl, toss together all the filling ingredients. Set aside.
2. Preheat the oven to 325°F.
3. Grease and flour a 9" X 5" loaf pan.
4. To make the cake, in a large bowl, cream the butter or margarine with the sugar until the sugar is fully incorporated. Beat in the eggs, then the vanilla.
5. In another bowl, stir together the flour, baking powder, and salt. Add to the creamed mixture, stirring until the dry ingredients are incorporated.
6. Spread one-third of the batter evenly in the prepared pan. Sprinkle with half the filling. Repeat the layers, and top with the final one-third of the batter.
7. Bake the cake for 1³/₄ hours or until a toothpick inserted in the center comes out clean. Transfer the pan to a rack to cool.

*Preparation time: 30 minutes*
*Yield: 12 to 14 servings*

# Raisin Pound Cake

This is one of the best butter cakes I've made. It is rich, fragrant with spices, and flecked through-out with dark and golden raisins. The addition of grated apple helps this cake stay fresh for days.

2 sticks (1 cup) butter or margarine, softened (try to use at least half butter)
1 cup sugar
1 cup brown sugar, preferably dark
4 eggs
Grated rind 1 orange
1 cup grated, peeled apple (about 2 medium-size apples)
2 cups flour
1 teaspoon baking powder
1 teaspoon ginger
¼ teaspoon nutmeg
¼ teaspoon cinnamon
1 cup dark raisins
1 cup golden raisins

1. Preheat the oven to 375°F.
2. Grease and flour a tube pan.
3. In a large bowl, cream the butter or margarine with the sugar and brown sugar until the sugars are fully incorporated. Beat in the eggs, then the orange rind and grated apple.
4. In another bowl, stir together the flour, baking

powder, ginger, nutmeg, and cinnamon. Add to the creamed mixture, stirring just until the dry ingredients are incorporated. Stir in the dark raisins and golden raisins.

5. Spread the batter in the prepared pan. Bake the cake for 25 minutes. Then lower the oven temperature to 325°F, and bake the cake for another 1 hour 10 minutes or until a toothpick inserted in the highest part of the cake comes out clean. Transfer the pan to a rack to cool.

*Preparation time: 30 minutes*
*Yield: 16 servings*

# Apricot Pound Cake

This lovely pound cake's delicate flavor and color are provided by pureed apricots, and the flavor is enhanced by soaking dried apricots in brandy. The cake keeps fresh longer than most pound cakes.

¼ **cup finely chopped dried apricots**
¼ **cup brandy**
2 **sticks (1 cup) butter or margarine, softened (try to use at least half butter)**
2 **cups sugar**
4 **eggs**
1 **16 ounce can apricot halves, drained and pureed in a food processor or blender**
½ **cup sour cream**
2 **teaspoons vanilla**
3 **cups flour**
½ **teaspoon baking soda**
¼ **teaspoon salt**

1. In a small bowl, combine the dried apricots and brandy. Set aside.
2. Preheat the oven to 325°F.
3. Grease and flour a tube pan.
4. In a large bowl, cream the butter or margarine with the sugar until the sugar is fully incorporated. Beat in the eggs, then the pureed apri-

cots, sour cream, and vanilla.

5. In another bowl, stir together the flour, baking soda, and salt. Add to the creamed mixture, stirring until the dry ingredients are incorporated. Stir in the dried apricots and any brandy that wasn't absorbed by them.

6. Turn the batter out into the prepared pan. Bake the cake for 1¾ hours or until a toothpick inserted in the highest part of the cake comes out clean. Transfer the pan to a rack to cool.

*Preparation time: 30 minutes*
*Yield: 18 to 20 servings*

# Streusel-Topped Butter Cake

Chapter 2, "Chocolate Forever," contains a recipe for chocolate cake that's enhanced by a raspberry-meringue filling. This cake uses the same technique and adds a crunchy oat-and-nut topping to make it even more enticing. If you like rich sour cream cakes for brunch, this one's a winner. It also makes a good family-style dessert, especially when topped with a scoop of ice cream. The cake may be served warm from the oven or at room temperature.

## FILLING
- 1 egg white
- ⅓ cup seedless raspberry jam

## STREUSEL
- ¼ cup brown sugar, preferably dark
- 2 tablespoons rolled oats
- ½ teaspoon cinnamon
- 2 teaspoons butter or margarine, softened
- 2 tablespoons chopped pecans

## CAKE
- 1½ sticks (¾ cup) butter or margarine, softened
- 1½ cups sugar
- 3 eggs plus 1 egg yolk
- 1 cup sour cream
- ½ cup milk
- 1½ teaspoons vanilla
- 1½ cups flour

    1   **cup whole-wheat flour**
  1$^1/_2$  **teaspoons baking powder**
    1   **teaspoon baking soda**
  $^1/_4$  **teaspoon salt**

1. To make the filling, beat the egg white until stiff. Beat in the raspberry jam. Set aside.
2. To make the streusel, mix all the streusel ingredients together with your fingertips until crumbly. Set aside.
3. Preheat the oven to 350°F.
4. Grease and flour a 9" x 13" baking pan.
5. To make the cake, in a large bowl, cream the butter or margarine with the sugar until the sugar is fully incorporated. Beat in the eggs and egg yolk, then the sour cream, milk, and vanilla.
6. In another bowl, stir together the flour, whole-wheat flour, baking powder, baking soda, and salt. Add to the creamed mixture, stirring until the dry ingredients are incorporated.
7. Spread half the batter evenly in the prepared pan. Sprinkle with half the streusel mixture. Using a teaspoon, drop dollops of the raspberry meringue over the streusel. (It won't completely cover the cake.) Spread the remaining batter evenly over the meringue, and sprinkle with the remaining streusel.
8. Bake the cake for 50 minutes or until a toothpick inserted in the center comes out clean. Transfer the pan to a rack to cool.

*Preparation time: 30 minutes*
*Yield: 16 servings*

# Coffee Liqueur Cake

This sour-cream pound cake is flavored with coffee liqueur. A spiced walnut filling ribbons through the cake, adding attractiveness and appeal. You could serve this cake for a brunch, accompanied by a fresh fruit salad. Or try drizzling it with Dark Chocolate Glaze (page 341) and topping each slice with a scoop of chocolate ice cream and a sprinkling of cinnamon.

## FILLING
- $1/3$ **cup brown sugar, preferably dark**
- $1/3$ **cup chopped walnuts**
- $1/4$ **teaspoon cinnamon**
- $1/4$ **teaspoon nutmeg**

## CAKE
- $1^1/2$ **sticks ($3/4$ cup) butter or margarine, softened (try to use at least half butter)**
- $1^3/4$ **cups sugar**
- 3 **eggs**
- 1 **cup sour cream**
- 1 **cup coffee liqueur**
- $1^1/2$ **teaspoons vanilla**
- 3 **cups flour**
- $1^1/2$ **teaspoons baking powder**
- $3/4$ **teaspoon baking soda**
- $1/4$ **teaspoon salt**

1. To make the filling, in a small bowl, mix together all the filling ingredients. Set aside.
2. Preheat the oven to 350°F.
3. Grease and flour a tube pan.
4. In a large bowl, cream the butter or margarine with the sugar until the sugar is fully incorporated. Beat in the eggs, then the sour cream, coffee liqueur, and vanilla.
5. In another bowl, stir together the flour, baking powder, baking soda, and salt. Add to the creamed mixture, stirring until the dry ingredients are incorporated.
6. Spread one-third of the batter evenly in the prepared pan. Sprinkle with half the filling mixture. Repeat. Spread the final third of the batter on top.
7. Bake the cake for $1\frac{1}{4}$ hours or until a toothpick inserted in the highest part of the cake comes out clean. Transfer the pan to a rack to cool.

*Preparation time: 25 minutes*
*Yield: 20 servings*

# Black Russian Cake

The addition of coffee liqueur, vodka, and a subtle quantity of chocolate makes this cake reminiscent of a Black Russian cocktail. This is a rich but light dessert that you'll want both to share and to savor yourself — perhaps accompanied by a frothy cappuccino. The cake also ships very well, making a most welcome "care package" for adults.

   2 sticks (1 cup) butter or margarine, softened
2¼ cups sugar
   5 eggs
⅓ cup coffee liqueur
⅓ cup vodka
   6 ounces (1 cup) semisweet chocolate morsels, melted
1¼ cups buttermilk or 4 teaspoons vinegar in a measuring cup plus milk up to the 1¼-cup mark
2¾ cups flour
¾ teaspoon baking soda
   1 teaspoon baking powder

1. Preheat the oven to 350°F.
2. Grease and flour a tube pan.
3. In a large bowl, cream the butter or margarine with the sugar until the sugar is fully incorporated. Beat in the eggs, then the coffee liqueur,

vodka, melted chocolate, and buttermilk.

4. In another bowl, stir together the flour, baking soda, and baking powder. Add to the creamed mixture, stirring until the dry ingredients are incorporated.

5. Turn the batter out into the prepared pan. Bake the cake for 1½ hours or until a toothpick inserted in the highest part of the cake comes out clean. Transfer the pan to a rack to cool.

*Preparation time: 25 minutes*
*Yield: 20 servings*

# Bourbon Pound Cake

A true pound cake calls for no liquid, making it very dense. The bourbon in this cake lightens the texture, not to mention adding a wonderfully heady flavor and aroma. This is one of the easiest and fastest cakes in this book to prepare.

        2  sticks (1 cup) butter or margarine,
           softened (try to use at least half
           butter)
    1²/₃  cups sugar
        5  eggs
        1  cup bourbon
        3  cups flour
        2  teaspoons baking powder
      ¹/₂  teaspoon nutmeg
      ¹/₄  teaspoon salt
        1  cup finely ground walnuts


1. Preheat the oven to 300°F.
2. Grease and flour a tube pan.
3. In a large bowl, cream the butter or margarine with the sugar until the sugar is fully incorporated. Beat in the eggs, then the bourbon.
4. In another bowl, stir together the flour, baking powder, nutmeg, and salt. Add to the creamed mixture, stirring just until the dry ingredients are incorporated. Stir in the walnuts.
5. Turn the batter out into the prepared pan. Bake the cake for 1³/₄ hours or until a toothpick

inserted in the highest part of the cake comes out clean. Transfer the pan to a rack to cool.

*Preparation time: 20 minutes*
*Yield: 18 to 20 servings*

# Ribbons-of-Chocolate Cake

This is a classic marble pound cake with extra chocolate added to the dark batter. It's the kind of old-fashioned homey cake that is loved by just about everyone. To bring out the chocolate flavor more fully, drizzle the cake with Dark Chocolate Glaze (page 341).

$2$   **sticks (1 cup) butter or margarine, softened (try to use at least half butter)**
$1^2/_3$   **cups sugar**
$5$   **eggs**
$2$   **teaspoons vanilla**
$1^1/_2$   **teaspoons almond extract**
$2^1/_3$   **cups flour**
$1^1/_2$   **teaspoons baking powder**
$^1/_8$   **teaspoon salt**
$^1/_2$   **cup semisweet chocolate morsels, melted**
$^1/_2$   **cup semisweet chocolate morsels, finely chopped**

1. Preheat the oven to 325°F.
2. Grease and flour a tube pan.
3. In a large bowl, cream the butter or margarine with the sugar until the sugar is fully incorporated. Beat in the eggs, then the vanilla and almond extract.
4. In another bowl, stir together the flour, baking

powder, and salt. Add to the creamed mixture, stirring just until the dry ingredients are incorporated.

5. Transfer about 1¹/₂ cups of the batter to another bowl. Stir in the melted chocolate and finely chopped chocolate.

6. Drop several heaping tablespoons of the plain batter into the prepared pan. Cover with some of the chocolate batter. Continue alternating batters in this fashion until all the batter has been used. Smooth the top of the cake. Run a knife through the batter to marbleize it, but do this only a few times since you don't want to mix the two batters together.

7. Bake the cake for 1 hour 10 minutes or until a toothpick inserted in the highest part of the cake comes out clean. Transfer the pan to a rack to cool.

*Preparation time: 25 minutes*
*Yield: 14 to 16 servings*

# Whipped Cream Pound Cake

This cake is different from the usual pound cake because whipped cream replaces the butter (which is made from heavy cream), thus maintaining the traditional butter-cake flavor but making the texture much lighter. Almonds both on the outside of the cake and in the batter lend a pleasant crunch, while a sweet orange glaze adds to the cake's attractiveness.

## CAKE
- $^1/_3$ cup finely chopped almonds for the pan plus $^1/_3$ cup chopped almonds for the cake
- 1 cup heavy cream or whipping cream
- 1 cup sugar
- 2 eggs
- $^1/_2$ teaspoon vanilla
- $^1/_4$ teaspoon almond extract
- $1^1/_2$ cups flour
- 2 teaspoons baking powder
- $^1/_8$ teaspoon salt

## GLAZE
- $2^1/_2$ tablespoons orange liqueur (such as Cointreau)
- 2 tablespoons sugar

1. Preheat the oven to 350°F.
2. Grease a 9" X 5" loaf pan, preferably with

butter. (Do *not* flour the pan.) Add the finely chopped almonds to the pan, tilting the pan so that the nuts evenly coat the bottom and sides.

3. To make the cake, in a large bowl, beat the cream until it is the consistency of whipped cream. (Use an electric mixer, not a food processor, for this.) Beat in the sugar, then the eggs, vanilla, and almond extract.

4. In another bowl, stir together the flour, baking powder, and salt. Add to the whipped-cream mixture, stirring just until the dry ingredients are incorporated. Stir in the chopped almonds.

5. Spread the batter evenly in the prepared pan, and bake the cake for 1 hour 5 minutes or until a toothpick inserted in the center comes out clean.

6. While the cake is baking, make the glaze. Heat the orange liqueur and sugar in a small saucepan, stirring until the sugar is dissolved.

7. As soon as the cake comes out of the oven, spoon the glaze evenly over the top. Transfer the pan to a rack to cool.

*Preparation time: 30 minutes*
*Yield: 10 servings*

# CHAPTER TWO

# CHOCOLATE FOREVER

Chocolate can be addictive. Those of us who have a passion for chocolate have very real cravings for it that go far beyond any need to appease hunger pangs. And while it's possible to develop yearnings for other favorite edibles (cheeseburgers, potato chips, pizza), these longings are rarely as intense — or as long-lived — as the chocoholic's nearly insatiable appetite for the velvety smooth taste of chocolate, whether it be in deep, dark brownies, meltingly rich fudge candy, or icy-cold chocolate ice cream.

I have met a few people who don't care for chocolate as well as others who are perfectly happy to eat it but equally satisfied with a different dessert. And it is difficult to relate to what those people are actually tasting. (I continue to remain astounded, for example, every time my husband orders apple pie in a restaurant when chocolate layer cake is also available.)

For those of us who are chocolate "addicts," no other flavor will suffice. If we want a brownie, it's because we long for that almost indescribable flavor; a butterscotch blondie is simply no substitute. If it's a hot-fudge sundae that we yearn for, an ice-cream topping in any other flavor is just a waste of calories. And if it's fudge cake that gets lodged in our mind as the craving to be satisfied, carrot cake can't possibly do the trick. "Chocolate Forever" is about indulgence. The cakes in this chapter are for people who, like me, truly desire chocolate. I offer here a wide selection for the chocolate fanatic (and others) — from a marble cake that weaves the chocolate through a buttery vanilla batter to cakes that are intense and fudgy throughout. There are also many cakes that add other wonderful ingredients — coffee, orange, cream cheese, nuts — to enhance, but never dilute, the basic chocolate flavor.

# Ultramoist Chocolate Pan Cake

This cake is a chocoholic's dream — it is rich and chocolaty, it is quick to put together, and it can be enjoyed right from the oven. If guilt isn't a concern, top a good-sized square of the cake with vanilla ice cream and a generous portion of Fudge Sauce (page 344).

*Note:* You may use just about any liqueur for this cake, including coffee, almond, hazelnut, coconut, orange, or mint. If, however, you don't want to introduce a new flavor, use chocolate liqueur.

## CAKE
- 2 sticks (1 cup) plus 2 tablespoons butter or margarine, softened
- $2^2/_3$ cups sugar
- 4 eggs
- 6 1-ounce squares unsweetened chocolate, melted
- 2 teaspoons vanilla
- 2 cups milk
- $3^1/_4$ cups flour
- $1^1/_2$ teaspoons baking powder
- 1 teaspoon baking soda
- $^1/_4$ teaspoon salt

## SYRUP
- $^1/_2$ cup water
- $^1/_4$ cup sugar
- $^1/_4$ cup liqueur of your choice (see *Note,* above)

1. Preheat oven to 325°F.
2. Grease and flour a 9" X 13" baking pan.
3. To make the cake, in a large bowl, cream the butter or margarine with the sugar until the sugar is fully incorporated. Beat in the eggs, then the chocolate, vanilla, and milk.
4. In another bowl, stir together the flour, baking powder, baking soda, and salt. Add to the chocolate mixture, stirring until the dry ingredients are incorporated.
5. Turn the batter out into the prepared pan. Bake the cake for $1\frac{1}{4}$ hours or until a toothpick inserted in the center comes out clean.
6. While the cake is baking, make the syrup. Bring the water and sugar to a boil, stirring until the sugar is dissolved. Remove the pan from the heat, and stir in the liqueur.
7. As soon as the cake comes out of the oven, prick it in about 12 to 15 places with the tines of a fork, and slowly pour the syrup over it. Transfer the pan to a rack to cool.

*Preparation time: 30 minutes*
*Yield: 24 servings*

# Two-Pound Chocolate Bars

Each Christmas, our next-door neighbor, Rose, brings over a lovely plate of assorted cookies. One year, the assortment included the fudgiest cookies I had ever tasted. They were so good that I hid them from my husband and daughter and ate them all myself. I atoned for this act by immediately asking Rose for the recipe, knowing that within just a few days, I'd be making an entire batch of these wonderful cookies and, of course, would dole out a few to my family. My cookies were as delicious as those baked by Rose, but her recipe was tedious to follow. The dough, containing only 1/4 cup of flour, was sticky and had to be formed into logs and chilled. I was determined to take the same ingredients and turn them into a far-easier-to-prepare bar version of the cookies. These Two-Pound Chocolate Bars (so named because they call for a full two pounds of chocolate!) are extraordinary — the most intensely chocolate dessert imaginable.

    1   **pound semisweet chocolate**
    1/2 **stick (4 tablespoons) butter**
        **or margarine**
    4   **eggs**
    1 1/2 **cups sugar**
    1   **tablespoon vanilla**
    1   **tablespoon instant coffee powder,**
        **dissolved in 1 teaspoon water**
    1/4 **cup flour**

1 teaspoon **baking powder**
$^1/_8$ **teaspoon salt**
1 **pound (2$^1/_2$ cups) semisweet chocolate, processed in the food processor to make large chunks, or semisweet chocolate morsels**

1. In a saucepan, melt the 1 pound semisweet chocolate with the butter, stirring occasionally.
2. Preheat the oven to 350°F.
3. Grease and flour a 9" x 13" baking pan.
4. In a large bowl, beat the eggs. Gradually beat in the sugar until the mixture is thick and pale. Beat in the melted chocolate, vanilla, and dissolved coffee.
5. In a small bowl, stir together the flour, baking powder, and salt. Add to the chocolate mixture, stirring until the dry ingredients are incorporated. Stir in the chocolate chunks or morsels.
6. Spread the batter evenly in the prepared pan. Bake the bars for 25 to 30 minutes. The bars will be shiny on top, and a toothpick inserted in the center will come out almost, but not completely, clean. Transfer the pan to a rack to cool. When cool, cut into bars.

*Preparation time: 25 minutes*
*Yield: 32 bars*

# Fudge-Fudge Cake

This recipe takes the classic marble cake and makes it even better, especially for those of us who crave chocolate. Instead of beginning with the usual vanilla cake batter, fudgy chocolate is the basic batter for this cake. Then a portion of the batter is enhanced with yet more chocolate as well as honey and coffee. The result is a cake so dark and chocolaty, you have to look hard to see the marbling. Serve the cake alone or, for pure ecstasy, with a scoop of ice cream.

## MARBLING MIXTURE
- ¼ cup unsweetened cocoa powder
- 2 tablespoons sugar
- 2 tablespoons honey
- 2 tablespoons coffee liqueur
- 2 tablespoons water
- 1 teaspoon instant coffee powder
- ⅛ teaspoon baking soda

## CAKE
- 2 sticks (1 cup) butter or margarine, softened
- 1¾ cups sugar
- 3 eggs
- ½ cup milk
- 2 teaspoons vanilla
- 2 cups flour
- 2 teaspoons baking powder
- ½ cup unsweetened cocoa powder, sifted if lumpy

1. To make the marbling mixture, in a small saucepan, combine all the ingredients except the baking soda. Bring to a boil, stirring constantly. Remove from the heat, and let cool slightly. Stir in the baking soda. Set aside.
2. Preheat the oven to 325°F.
3. Grease and flour a tube pan.
4. To make the cake, in a large bowl, cream the butter or margarine with the sugar until the sugar is fully incorporated. Beat in the eggs, then the milk and vanilla.
5. In another bowl, stir together the flour, baking powder, and cocoa. Add to the creamed mixture, stirring until the dry ingredients are incorporated.
6. Remove about one-third of the cake batter to another bowl and stir in the marbling mixture.
7. Place several spoonfuls of the lighter chocolate batter in the prepared pan. Cover with several spoonfuls of the darker batter. Continue alternating batters in this fashion until all batter has been used. Run a knife through the batters to marbleize them, but do it only a few times since you don't want to mix the two batters together.
8. Bake the cake for $1^{1}/_{4}$ hours or until a toothpick inserted in the highest part of the cake comes out clean. Transfer the pan to a rack to cool.

*Preparation time: 30 minutes*
*Yield: 16 servings*

# Chocolate–Sour Cream Layer Cake

The addition of sour cream makes cakes that are light in texture yet richly flavored, and this chocolate cake is no exception. It's especially delicious when the layers are sandwiched together with Chocolate Cream Filling (page 342).

*Note:* I find that the filling between the layers provides ample additional sweetness. But if you love frosting, by all means, frost the top and sides of the cake as well. The Chocolate Butter Frosting (page 339) would work well.

|   |   |
|---|---|
| 1 | stick (½ cup) butter or margarine, softened |
| 2 | cups sugar |
| 2 | eggs |
| 1 | cup sour cream |
| 1 | teaspoon vanilla |
| 3 | cups flour |
| ¾ | cup unsweetened cocoa powder, sifted if lumpy |
| 1½ | teaspoons baking powder |
| ½ | teaspoon baking soda |
| ¼ | teaspoon salt |
|   | Chocolate Cream Filling (see page 342) |

1. Preheat the oven to 350°F.
2. Grease and flour two 9" round layer-cake pans.

3. In a large bowl, cream the butter or margarine with the sugar until the sugar is fully incorporated. Beat in the eggs, then the sour cream and vanilla.
4. In another bowl, stir together the flour, cocoa, baking powder, baking soda, and salt. Add to the creamed mixture, stirring until the dry ingredients are incorporated.
5. Divide the batter evenly between the prepared pans. Bake the cake layers for 30 minutes or until a toothpick inserted in the center of each layer comes out clean. Transfer the pans to a rack to cool.
6. When cool, remove the layers from the pans. Place one layer on a serving plate top side up. Spread with the Chocolate Cream Filling. Place the second layer (also right side up) on top of the filling.

*Preparation time: 20 minutes*
*Yield: 12 servings*

# Chocolate Syrup Cake

My husband actually thought this cake was too chocolaty. But my daughter and I don't believe such a thing is possible. If you share this view, this cake is for you. What makes this cake unique is that a rich chocolate syrup is poured over the batter. As the cake bakes, the syrup seeps through the batter, making the cake incredibly fudgelike. A layer of thickened syrup also forms at the bottom of the pan. Altogether, this is a treat not to be missed by chocolate lovers.

*Note:* This cake should be served directly from the baking pan since the syrup will stick to the bottom if you try to remove the cake. Also, any leftovers should be stored in the refrigerator. For best flavor, bring the cake to room temperature before serving it.

## SYRUP

- 3  1-ounce squares unsweetened chocolate
- 1  cup water
- 1⅓  cups sugar
- 1  stick (½ cup) butter or margarine
- 2  teaspoons vanilla

## CAKE

- 11  tablespoons butter or margarine, softened
- 1⅓  cups sugar
- 2  eggs
- 1  cup milk
- 1  teaspoon vanilla
- 2  cups flour
- ½  cup unsweetened cocoa powder,

**sifted if lumpy**
2 **teaspoons baking powder**
¹/₄ **teaspoon salt**

1. To make the syrup, in a saucepan, heat the chocolate and water, stirring occasionally, until the
   chocolate has melted. Stir in the sugar, and bring
   to a boil, stirring occasionally. Remove from the
   heat, and add the butter or margarine. Stir occasionally until the butter has melted. Add the vanilla. Set aside.
2. Preheat the oven to 350°F.
3. Grease and flour a 9" square baking pan. Use a
   deep pan, such as a glass one made by Pyrex.
4. To make the cake, in a large bowl, cream the butter
   or margarine with the sugar until the sugar is fully
   incorporated. Beat in the eggs, then the milk and
   vanilla.
5. In another bowl, stir together the flour, cocoa,
   baking powder, and salt. Add to the creamed mixture, stirring until the dry ingredients are incorporated.
6. Spread the batter evenly in the prepared pan. Pour
   the syrup evenly over the batter. A little batter
   may rise over the top as the cake bakes, so place
   the pan on a baking sheet to protect the bottom
   of your oven.
7. Bake the cake for 1 hour 5 minutes or until the
   blade of a knife inserted anywhere in the cake
   except the center comes out clean. Transfer the
   pan to a rack to cool.

*Preparation time: 30 minutes*
*Yield: 16 servings*

73

# Chocolate Breakfast Cake

I could easily eat chocolate morning, noon, and night — and I bet I'm not alone. I developed this dense chocolate cake that's not too sweet, making it the perfect accompaniment to a morning cup of coffee. Like all chocolate cakes, this one is also delicious as a dessert, especially if you spread Chocolate–Sour Cream Icing (page 335) over the top.

1½ sticks (¾ cup) butter or margarine, softened
2 3-ounce packages cream cheese, softened
1½ cups sugar
2 eggs
¾ cup milk
2 teaspoons vanilla
1¾ cups flour
¾ cup unsweetened cocoa powder, sifted if lumpy
2 teaspoons baking powder
¼ teaspoon salt

1. Preheat the oven to 350°F.
2. Butter and flour a tube pan.
3. In a large bowl, cream the butter or margarine and cream cheese with the sugar until the sugar is fully incorporated. Beat in the eggs, then the milk and vanilla.

4. In another bowl, stir together the flour, cocoa, baking powder, and salt. Add to the creamed mixture, stirring until the dry ingredients are incorporated.
5. Turn the batter out into the prepared pan. Bake the cake for 1 hour or until a toothpick inserted in the highest part of the cake comes out clean. Transfer the pan to a rack to cool.

*Preparation time: 20 minutes*
*Yield: 12 to 14 servings*

# Mint Fudge Cake

Some people like the flavor of peppermint combined with chocolate almost as much as — or even more than — the taste of chocolate alone. This is the cake for them. It's dark and smooth, with a light airy texture. Although the cake does not call for butter, heavy cream and the high-fat content of the chocolate provide ample richness. Chocolate–Sour Cream Icing (page 335) goes well with this cake, especially if you add some peppermint extract (about ¼ teaspoon) to the icing just before spreading it.

- **10 ounces Hershey's Cookies 'n' Mint Nuggets**
- **2 1-ounce squares unsweetened chocolate**
- **1 cup heavy cream or whipping cream**
- **5 eggs**
- **½ cup sugar**
- **1 teaspoon vanilla**
- **¾ cup flour**
- **½ teaspoon baking soda**

1. In a saucepan over very low heat, melt the nuggets and chocolate in the cream. Stir until fully melted. Remove from the heat.
2. Preheat the oven to 325°F.
3. Grease and flour a 9" square baking pan.
4. In a large bowl, beat the eggs. Add the sugar

gradually, continuing to beat until the mixture is thick and creamy. Beat in the chocolate mixture and vanilla.

5. In another bowl, stir together the flour and baking soda. Add to the bowl with the chocolate mixture, stirring just until the dry ingredients are incorporated.

6. Turn the batter out into the prepared pan. Bake the cake for 50 to 60 minutes or until a toothpick inserted in the center comes out clean. Transfer the pan to a rack to cool.

*Preparation time: 25 minutes*
*Yield: 14 to 16 servings*

# Chocolate Liqueur Cake

Chocolate liqueur makes this cake especially dense and fudgy. Besides being versatile, this cake is so quick to put together that it's likely to become one of your most often-used desserts.

*Note:* In this recipe, you can use almost any flavor liqueur that's compatible with chocolate. Liqueurs that work especially well here are crème de menthe, coffee, orange, hazelnut, and amaretto.

| | |
|---|---|
| 1 | stick (½ cup) butter or margarine, softened |
| ¾ | cup sugar |
| 1 | cup brown sugar, preferably dark |
| 3 | eggs |
| 1 | tablespoon instant coffee powder, dissolved in ¾ cup water |
| ¾ | cup liqueur (see *Note,* above) |
| 2¼ | cups flour |
| ½ | cup unsweetened cocoa powder, sifted if lumpy |
| 1½ | teaspoons baking powder |
| ½ | cup mini-chocolate chips |

1. Preheat the oven to 350°F.
2. Grease and flour a tube pan.
3. In a large bowl, cream the butter or margarine with the sugar and brown sugar until the sugars are fully incorporated. Beat in the eggs,

then the coffee mixture and the liqueur.

4. In another bowl, stir together the flour, cocoa, and baking powder. Add to the creamed mixture, stirring just until the dry ingredients are incorporated. Stir in the chocolate chips.

5. Turn the batter out into the prepared pan. Bake the cake for 1 hour 5 minutes or until a toothpick inserted in the highest part of the cake comes out clean. Transfer the pan to a rack to cool.

*Preparation time: 20 minutes*
*Yield: 12 to 16 servings*

# Chocolate–Chocolate Chip Fruitcake

This fruitcake contains no candied fruits. Rather, the cake is filled with dates, apricots, and golden raisins. The addition of chocolate to the batter and chocolate chips scattered throughout make it the perfect holiday dessert for chocoholics. The cake keeps well and is a good choice for shipping.

|   |   |
|---|---|
| 2 | sticks (1 cup) butter or margarine, softened |
| 1½ | cups brown sugar, preferably dark |
| 3 | eggs |
| ½ | cup water |
| ½ | cup coffee liqueur |
| 2¼ | cups flour |
| ¾ | cup unsweetened cocoa powder, sifted if lumpy |
| 2 | teaspoons baking powder |
| ¼ | teaspoon salt |
| 6 | ounces (about 1 cup) semisweet chocolate morsels |
| 8 | ounces (about 1½ cups) chopped dates |
| 8 | ounces (about 1½ cups) chopped dried apricots |
| ½ | cup golden raisins |
| 1½ | cups chopped walnuts |

1. Preheat the oven to 350°F.
2. Grease and flour a tube pan.
3. In a large bowl, cream the butter or margarine with the sugar until the sugar is fully incorporated. Beat in the eggs, then the water and coffee liqueur.
4. In another bowl, stir together the flour, cocoa, baking powder, and salt. Add to the creamed mixture, stirring until the dry ingredients are incorporated. Stir in the chocolate, dates, apricots, raisins, and walnuts.
5. Turn the batter out into the prepared pan. Bake the cake for 1 hour 50 minutes or until a toothpick inserted in the highest part of the cake comes out clean. Transfer the pan to a rack to cool.

*Preparation time: 30 minutes*
*Yield: 20 to 24 servings*

# Ribbon-of-Raspberry Cake

This is a good, basic chocolate cake with a surprise filling — raspberry-flavored meringue — which lends a sweet textural contrast and fruity taste. If you're a fan of raspberry-filled chocolate bonbons, you'll love this. The Dark Chocolate Glaze (page 341) adds to the cake's appeal.

## FILLING
    1   egg white
    1/3 cup seedless raspberry jam

## CAKE
    1 1/2   sticks (3/4 cup) butter or margarine, softened
    1 3/4   cups sugar
    2   eggs plus 1 egg yolk
    1   teaspoon vanilla
    1 1/3   cups water
    2   cups flour
    3/4   cup unsweetened cocoa powder, sifted if lumpy
    1 1/2   teaspoons baking powder
    1/4   teaspoon salt

1. To make the filling, in a small bowl, beat the egg white until stiff. Beat in the raspberry jam. Set aside.
2. Preheat the oven to 350°F.
3. Grease and flour a 9" x 13" baking pan.

4. To make the cake, in a large bowl, cream the butter or margarine with the sugar until the sugar is fully incorporated. Beat in the eggs and egg yolk, then the vanilla and water.
5. In another bowl, stir together the flour, cocoa, baking powder, and salt. Add to the creamed mixture, stirring until the dry ingredients are incorporated.
6. Spread half the batter evenly in the prepared pan. Spread the meringue as evenly as possible over the batter. Cover with the remaining batter.
7. Bake the cake for 40 minutes or until a toothpick inserted in the center comes out clean. Transfer the pan to a rack to cool.

*Preparation time: 30 minutes*
*Yield: 15 servings*

# Chocolate-Jam Cake

This is a very rich chocolate–sour cream pound cake that's enhanced by whatever flavor jam you choose. Apricot, raspberry, or cherry jam as well as orange marmalade are all excellent choices. If you like the contrast of chocolate cake covered with vanilla frosting, try the Creamy White Icing (page 334) here.

| | |
|---|---|
| 10 | tablespoons butter or margarine, softened |
| 1½ | cups sugar |
| 2 | eggs |
| 2 | cups sour cream |
| 1 | teaspoon vanilla |
| ¾ | cup jam or preserves |
| 2 | cups flour |
| ¾ | cup unsweetened cocoa powder, sifted if lumpy |
| 1 | teaspoon baking soda |
| ¼ | teaspoon salt |

1. Preheat the oven to 350°F.
2. Grease and flour a tube pan.
3. In a large bowl, cream the butter or margarine with the sugar until the sugar is fully incorporated. Beat in the eggs, then the sour cream, vanilla, and jam.
4. In another bowl, stir together the flour, cocoa, baking soda, and salt. Add to the creamed

mixture, stirring until the dry ingredients are incorporated.

5. Turn the batter out into the prepared pan. Bake the cake for 1½ hours or until a toothpick inserted in the highest part of the cake comes out clean. Transfer the pan to a rack to cool.

*Preparation time: 20 minutes*
*Yield: 12 to 14 servings*

# Brownie Macaroon "Pie"

For fans of chocolate and coconut, this dessert is a must. The crust is like a large chewy macaroon, while the filling is a very rich chocolate brownie. Cut the "pie" into thin wedges, and serve it plain. Or, for a special treat, top each portion with vanilla ice cream and Fudge Sauce (page 344).

## CRUST

- 2 egg whites
- $\frac{1}{3}$ cup sugar
- 2 cups sweetened flaked coconut
- 2 tablespoons flour

## FILLING

- 1 stick ($\frac{1}{2}$ cup) butter or margarine
- 2 1-ounce squares unsweetened chocolate
- 2 ounces semisweet chocolate
- 2 eggs
- 1 cup brown sugar, preferably dark
- $\frac{1}{2}$ cup sugar
- 1 teaspoon vanilla
- 1 cup flour
- 1 teaspoon baking powder
- $\frac{1}{8}$ teaspoon salt

1. Preheat the oven to 375°F.
2. Grease and flour a 9" deep-dish pie plate.
3. To make the crust, beat the egg whites with

the sugar until foamy. (Do *not* beat until stiff peaks form.) Beat in the coconut and flour. Spread the mixture evenly on the bottom and sides of the prepared pan.

4. Bake the crust for 10 minutes.
5. While the crust is baking, make the filling. In a saucepan, melt the butter or margarine with the unsweetened chocolate and semisweet chocolate over a very low heat, stirring occasionally. Remove from the heat.
6. In a large bowl, beat the eggs. Gradually beat in the brown sugar and sugar until the mixture is thick. Beat in the chocolate mixture, then the vanilla.
7. In another bowl, stir together the flour, baking powder, and salt. Add to the chocolate mixture, stirring just until the dry ingredients are incorporated.
8. Spread the filling in the pie crust. Return the pie to the oven, and bake 25 minutes longer or until a toothpick inserted in the center comes out clean. Transfer the pie plate to a rack to cool.

*Preparation time: 30 minutes*
*Yield: 8 to 10 servings*

# Dark and White Chocolate Cake

If ever there were a "perfect cake," Dark and White Chocolate Cake would be a contender for the prize. Although the white chocolate doesn't contribute a chocolate flavor, it does lend an incredibly smooth, rich quality to the batter. Chocolate chips are scattered throughout the cake; to accentuate this chocolate favor, cover the cake with Chocolate Butter Frosting (page 339).

2 sticks (1 cup) butter or margarine (try to use at least half butter)
3 1-ounce squares white baking chocolate
3 eggs
1²/₃ cups sugar
1 cup buttermilk or 1 tablespoon lemon juice in a measuring cup plus milk up to the 1-cup mark
2 teaspoons vanilla
2¹/₃ cups flour
³/₄ teaspoon baking soda
2 teaspoons baking powder
¹/₈ teaspoon salt
1 cup mini-chocolate chips

1. In a saucepan, melt the butter or margarine and white chocolate over a very low heat, stirring occasionally. Remove from the heat.
2. Preheat the oven to 350°F.

3. Grease and flour a tube pan.
4. In a large bowl, beat the eggs. Gradually beat in the sugar until the mixture is thick and pale yellow. Beat in the chocolate mixture, then the buttermilk and vanilla.
5. In another bowl, stir together the flour, baking soda, baking powder, and salt. Add to the egg mixture, stirring until the dry ingredients are incorporated. Stir in the chocolate chips.
6. Turn the batter out into the prepared pan. Bake the cake for 1 hour 10 minutes or until a toothpick inserted in the highest part of the cake comes out clean. Transfer the pan to a rack to cool.

*Preparation time: 25 minutes*
*Yield: 16 servings*

# Cookie-Crust Chocolate Cake

If you like cookie-crumb crusts on cheesecakes but aren't crazy about the filling, this recipe is for you. For instead of being baked in the usual metal cake pan, this chocolate-nut graham cracker crust is baked in a pie plate and is used to hold the cake batter. The result is a fabulously chocolaty cake that looks like a pie and is great on its own or with a scoop of ice cream.

## CRUST
- 1½ cups graham cracker crumbs
- ½ cup brown sugar, preferably dark
- ½ cup finely chopped pecans
- ¼ cup unsweetened cocoa powder, sifted if lumpy
- ½ stick (4 tablespoons) butter or margarine, melted

## CAKE
- 1½ sticks (¾ cup) butter or margarine, softened
- ¾ cup brown sugar, preferably dark
- 3 eggs
- 1½ cups chocolate syrup
- ¾ teaspoon vanilla
- 1½ cups flour
- 3 tablespoons unsweetened cocoa powder, sifted if lumpy
- 1½ teaspoons baking powder
- ⅓ cup chopped pecans

1. To make the crust, stir together all the crust ingredients, and press into the bottom and a little up the sides of a greased 9" or 10" pie plate. Set aside.
2. Preheat the oven to 350°F.
3. To make the cake, in a large bowl, cream the butter or margarine with the brown sugar until the sugar is fully incorporated. Beat in the eggs, then the chocolate syrup and vanilla.
4. In another bowl, stir together the flour, cocoa, and baking powder. Add to the creamed mixture, stirring until the dry ingredients are incorporated. Stir in the pecans.
5. Spread the batter evenly in the prepared pan. Bake the cake for 1 hour or until a toothpick inserted in the center comes out clean. Transfer the pan to a rack to cool.

*Preparation time: 30 minutes*
*Yield: 10 to 12 servings*

# Cheesecake Chocolate Cake

For those who dote on chocolate cake <u>and</u> cheese-cake, this dessert satisfies both cravings at once. Rich chocolate-cake batter is topped with a creamy cheesecake mixture. Both are baked together to create a two-layer delight.
*Note:* Leftovers should be refrigerated.

## CHEESECAKE MIXTURE
- 1  8-ounce package cream cheese, softened
- 2  tablespoons butter or margarine, softened
- 1  14-ounce can sweetened condensed milk (not evaporated milk)
- 1  egg
- 2  tablespoons  water
- 2  teaspoons vanilla

## CAKE
- 4  1-ounce squares unsweetened chocolate
- $^1/_2$  cup plus $1^1/_4$ cups sugar, divided
- $^2/_3$  cup water
- 1  stick ($^1/_2$ cup) butter or margarine, softened
- 3  eggs
- $^3/_4$  cup milk
- 2  teaspoons vanilla
- $1^2/_3$  cups flour
- 1  teaspoon baking powder

¹/₂ **teaspoon baking soda**
¹/₈ **teaspoon salt**

1. To make the cheesecake mixture, in a large bowl, beat together all the cheesecake ingredients until thoroughly mixed. Set aside.
2. To make the cake, in a small saucepan, melt the chocolate with the ¹/₂ cup of sugar and the water, stirring occasionally. Remove from the heat and set aside.
3. Preheat the oven to 350°F.
4. Grease and flour a 9" X 13" baking pan.
5. In a large bowl, cream the butter or margarine with the 1¹/₄ cups of sugar until the sugar is fully incorporated. Beat in the eggs, then the chocolate mixture, milk, and vanilla.
6. In another bowl, stir together the flour, baking powder, baking soda, and salt. Add to the chocolate mixture, stirring until the dry ingredients are incorporated.
7. Turn the batter out into the prepared pan. Gently spread the cheesecake mixture over the chocolate batter. Bake the cake for 1 hour or until a toothpick inserted in the center comes out clean. Transfer the pan to a rack to cool.

*Preparation time: 30 minutes*
*Yield: 16 servings*

# Chocolate–Cream Cheese Surprise Cake

Chocolate and cheesecake combine here in a single luscious dessert that has a layer of chocolate-chip cheesecake filling running through a velvety cake. If you're the kind of person who has trouble deciding whether to order the chocolate cake or the cheesecake when you're in a restaurant, this cake solves your problem.

*Note:* Leftovers should be stored in the refrigerator.

## FILLING
- 1 8-ounce package cream cheese, softened
- ¼ cup sugar
- 6 ounces (about 1 cup) mini-chocolate chips
- 1 teaspoon vanilla

## CAKE
- 2 eggs
- 2 cups sugar
- 2 sticks (1 cup) butter or margarine, melted
- 1 cup milk
- 1 cup water
- 1 teaspoon vanilla
- 3 cups flour
- ¾ cup unsweetened cocoa powder, sifted if lumpy

**2 teaspoons baking powder**
**¼ teaspoon salt**

1. To make the filling, in a small bowl, mix all the filling ingredients. Set aside.
2. Preheat the oven to 375°F.
3. Grease and flour a tube pan.
4. To make the cake, in a large bowl, beat the eggs. Gradually beat in the sugar until the mixture is thick and pale yellow. Beat in the melted butter or margarine, then the milk, water, and vanilla.
5. In another bowl, stir together the flour, cocoa, baking powder, and salt. Add to the egg mixture, stirring until the dry ingredients are incorporated.
6. Spread half the batter in the prepared pan. Using a teaspoon, drop spoonfuls of the filling evenly over the batter. Cover with the remaining batter.
7. Bake the cake for 1¼ hours or until a toothpick inserted in the highest part of the cake comes out clean. Transfer the pan to a rack to cool.

*Preparation time: 30 minutes*
*Yield: 16 to 20 servings*

# Double Chocolate Chip Cake

This is a rich sour cream butter cake that's filled with chocolate chips and then sprinkled with yet more chips before baking. It's delicious warm from the oven, especially if topped with a scoop of vanilla ice cream.

## TOPPING
- 2 tablespoons butter or margarine, softened
- ½ cup brown sugar, preferably dark
- 1 tablespoon flour
- ½ cup chopped walnuts
- 3 ounces (about ½ cup) semisweet chocolate morsels

## CAKE
- 1½ sticks (¾ cup) butter or margarine, softened
- 1½ cups sugar
- 4 eggs
- 1½ cups sour cream
- 1 teaspoon vanilla
- 3 cups flour
- 1 teaspoon baking powder
- 1 teaspoon baking soda
- ¼ teaspoon salt
- 9 ounces (about 1½ cups) semisweet chocolate morsels

1. To make the topping, in a small bowl, mix all the topping ingredients. Set aside.
2. Preheat the oven to 350°F.
3. Grease and flour a 9" X 13" baking pan.
4. To make the cake, in a large bowl, cream the butter or margarine with the sugar until the sugar is fully incorporated. Beat in the eggs, then the sour cream and vanilla.
5. In another bowl, stir together the flour, baking powder, baking soda, and salt. Add to the creamed mixture, stirring until the dry ingredients are incorporated. Stir in the chocolate.
6. Spread the batter evenly in the prepared pan. Sprinkle with the topping. Bake the cake for 45 to 50 minutes or until a toothpick inserted in the center comes out clean. Transfer the pan to a rack to cool.

*Preparation time: 25 minutes*
*Yield: 16 to 20 servings*

# CHAPTER THREE

# CAKES WITH FRUIT

After chocolate cake, cakes containing fresh fruits are my favorite. As each new season arrives, bringing with it its own marvelous variety of fruits, I dig out the recipes that I had been holding onto all those months, just waiting for these ingredients to make themselves available again. Thus, the end of summer finds me making lovely cakes with sensually dark Italian prune plums; fall has me buying bags of tart, brilliantly red cranberries for baking; and, as summer arrives, I rush to prepare homey cakes filled with tender, ripe peaches and beautiful, tangy blueberries. Apples, one of the most versatile fruits for cakes, fortunately can be purchased year round.

In almost all instances, it is far preferable to use fresh fruits in a cake recipe rather than canned or frozen ones. Perhaps the one exception is pineapple: canned pineapple, especially when packed in its juice, is fine in cakes and saves you the tedious job of preparing the fresh fruit. But there is no adequate substitute for fresh pears, peaches, blueberries, strawberries, or apples. (When a recipe calls for applesauce, however, the store-bought variety is convenient and acceptable.)

When you're making a cake that specifies fresh fruits, have the fruit ready to add to the batter before you begin the recipe. Many fruits require almost no effort to prepare: bananas need only be peeled and mashed; blueberries and cranberries are just washed and picked over; and plums are halved and pitted. Apples require the most preparation time. But, fortunately, since you need far fewer apples for cake batters than for pies or applesauce, even this step goes quickly.

This chapter also includes cakes that call for dried fruits, which have a pronounced flavor and an incomparable chewy quality. What's more, they are available all year, require virtually no preparation, and come in the same array of flavors as their fresh-fruit counterparts. Thus, you can choose to bake with dark and golden raisins, dates, figs, prunes, dried apricots, dried apples, dried pears, or more exotic fruits such as dried cranberries, cherries, or pineapple. Most fruits in most combinations will make for wonderfully delicious cakes.

# Fresh Apple Spice Cake

Raw apples and brandy (which has been both added to the batter and sprinkled over the baked cake) make for a flavorful dessert that keeps fresh for days. Serve the cake warm from the oven or at room temperature.

 2 sticks (1 cup) butter or margarine, softened
 2 cups sugar
 3 eggs
 ½ cup buttermilk or 1½ teaspoons vinegar in a measuring cup plus milk up to the ½-cup mark
 ¼ cup brandy plus additional ½ cup for drizzling on the finished cake
 1 teaspoon vanilla
 1½ cups flour
 1½ cups whole-wheat flour
 1 teaspoon baking soda
 1 teaspoon cinnamon
 ½ teaspoon nutmeg
 ¼ teaspoon ground cloves
 ¼ teaspoon salt
 2 cups unpeeled, cored, and coarsely chopped apples
 1 cup chopped walnuts

1. Preheat the oven to 350°F.
2. Grease and flour a 9" x 13" baking pan.

3. In a large bowl, cream the butter or margarine with the sugar until the sugar is fully incorporated. Beat in the eggs, then the buttermilk, ¼ cup of brandy, and vanilla.
4. In another bowl, stir together the flour, wholewheat flour, baking soda, cinnamon, nutmeg, cloves, and salt. Add to the creamed mixture, stirring until the dry ingredients are incorporated. Stir in the apples and walnuts.
5. Turn the batter out into the prepared pan. Bake the cake for 45 to 50 minutes or until a toothpick inserted in the center comes out clean. Transfer the pan to a rack to cool, and drizzle the cake with the remaining ½ cup of brandy.

*Preparation time: 30 minutes*
*Yield: 20 servings*

# Crumb-Topped Apple Cake

Like a giant, cinnamony apple muffin, this cake sandwiches a layer of sautéed apples in a vanilla batter that's sprinkled with a crunchy crumb topping. Since it's not too sweet, the cake is delicious with morning coffee or as a dessert for brunch.

**FILLING**
- 2 apples, peeled, cored, and sliced
- 2 tablespoons butter or margarine
- 2 tablespoons sugar
- 2 teaspoons cinnamon

**TOPPING**
- 1/4 cup brown sugar, preferably dark
- 1/2 stick  (4 tablespoons) butter or margarine, softened
- 1/4 cup flour
- 1/2 cup dry packaged unseasoned bread crumbs

**CAKE**
- 2 eggs
- 1 cup sugar
- 6 tablespoons butter or margarine, melted
- 1 1/3 cups milk
- 2 teaspoons vanilla
- 3 cups flour
- 4 teaspoons baking powder
- 1/4 teaspoon salt

1. To make the filling, in a skillet, sauté the apples in the butter or margarine until just tender. Stir in the sugar and cinnamon. Set aside.
2. To make the topping, in a small bowl, combine all the topping ingredients. Set aside.
3. Preheat the oven to 350°F.
4. Grease and flour a tube pan.
5. To make the cake, in a large bowl, beat the eggs. Gradually beat in the sugar until the mixture is thick and pale yellow. Beat in the melted butter or margarine, then the milk and vanilla.
6. In another bowl, stir together the flour, baking powder, and salt. Add to the egg mixture, stirring until the dry ingredients are incorporated.
7. Spread half the batter in the prepared pan. Spread the apple filling evenly over the batter, and cover with the remaining batter. Sprinkle with the crumb topping.
8. Bake the cake for 1 hour or until a toothpick inserted in the highest part of the cake comes out clean. Transfer the pan to a rack to cool.

*Preparation time: 30 minutes*
*Yield: 16 to 18 servings*

# Pear and Almond Cake

This cake has three luscious layers. The bottom is a rich lemon-flavored sour cream cake. The fresh pears in the next layer dissolve into a jamlike filling when the cake is baked. Finally, crunchy almonds become deliciously toasted in the macaroon topping. The cake is wonderfully refreshing, particularly when accompanied by a scoop of lemon sorbet.

## TOPPING
- ¾ cup sugar
- 1 tablespoon flour
- 2 tablespoons butter or margarine, softened
- 1 cup finely chopped almonds

## CAKE
- 1½ sticks (¾ cup) butter or margarine, softened
- 1½ cups sugar
- 4 eggs
- 1 teaspoon grated lemon peel
- 2 teaspoons vanilla
- 1 teaspoon almond extract
- 1 cup sour cream
- ½ cup milk
- 3 cups flour
- 1½ teaspoons baking powder
- 1 teaspoon baking soda
- ¼ teaspoon salt

**3 pears (ripe, but not overly soft),
peeled, cored, and thinly sliced**

1. To make the topping, in a small bowl, mix together all the topping ingredients. Set aside.
2. Preheat the oven to 350°F.
3. Grease and flour a 9" x 13" baking pan.
4. To make the cake, in a large bowl, cream the butter or margarine with the sugar until the sugar is fully incorporated. Beat in the eggs, then the lemon peel, vanilla, almond extract, sour cream, and milk.
5. In another bowl, stir together the flour, baking powder, baking soda, and salt. Add to the creamed mixture, stirring until the dry ingredients are incorporated.
6. Spread the batter evenly in the prepared pan. Distribute the pear slices evenly over the batter. Sprinkle the topping over the pears.
7. Bake the cake for 1½ hours or until a toothpick inserted in the center comes out clean. Transfer the pan to a rack to cool.

*Preparation time: 30 minutes*
*Yield: 16 to 20 servings*

# Blueberry Pound Cake

Blueberries bursting with dark sweet juice flavor a rich, buttery pound cake. This makes a lovely summer dessert for brunch and goes especially well with cappuccino or flavored coffees. Because blueberries require virtually no preparation, this is a very quick, easy cake to put together.

*Note:* This cake should be stored in the refrigerator. For best favor, bring it to room temperature before serving it.

> 2 **sticks (1 cup) butter or margarine, softened (try to use at least half butter)**
> 1²/₃ **cups sugar**
> 5 **eggs**
> 2 **tablespoons brandy**
> 2¹/₃ **cups flour**
> 1 **teaspoon baking powder**
> ¹/₄ **teaspoon salt**
> 2 **cups (1 pint) blueberries, rinsed and dried**

1. Preheat the oven to 300°F.
2. Grease and flour a tube pan.
3. In a large bowl, cream the butter or margarine with the sugar until the sugar is fully incorporated. Beat in the eggs, then the brandy.
4. In another bowl, stir together the flour, baking powder, and salt. Add to the creamed mixture, stirring until the dry ingredients are incorpo-

rated. Stir in the blueberries.

5. Turn the batter out into the prepared pan. Bake the cake for 1½ hours or until a toothpick inserted in the highest part of the cake comes out clean. Transfer the pan to a rack to cool.

*Preparation time: 20 minutes*
*Yield: 12 to 14 servings*

# Blueberry Cheesecake Cake

For people who like cake and cheesecake, this combines the best of both desserts. A simple vanilla cake is topped with blueberries and then covered with a ricotta-cheesecake mixture. The result is a blueberry cake with cheesecake "icing."

*Note:* This cake should be served cold and should be stored in the refrigerator.

**TOPPING**
- 2 eggs
- 1 15-ounce container ricotta
- 1/3 cup sugar
- 1/2 teaspoon vanilla

**CAKE**
- 1 stick (1/2 cup) butter or margarine, softened
- 1 1/2 cups sugar
- 2 eggs
- 2/3 cup milk
- 1 teaspoon vanilla
- 1 cup flour
- 1 cup whole-wheat flour
- 2 1/2 teaspoons baking powder
- 1/4 teaspoon salt
- 1 1/2 cups blueberries, rinsed and dried

1. To make the topping, in a small bowl, mix well all the topping ingredients. Set aside.

2. Preheat the oven to 350°F.
3. Grease and flour a 9" X 13" baking pan.
4. To make the cake, in a large bowl, cream the butter or margarine with the sugar until the sugar is fully incorporated. Beat in the eggs, then the milk and vanilla.
5. In another bowl, stir together the flour, whole-wheat flour, baking powder, and salt. Add to the creamed mixture, stirring until the dry ingredients are incorporated.
6. Spread the batter in the prepared pan. Sprinkle the blueberries over the batter. Spread the topping evenly over the berries.
7. Bake the cake for 55 to 60 minutes or until the topping is firm and set. Transfer the pan to a rack to cool. When cool, refrigerate the cake until ready to serve.

*Preparation time: 25 minutes*
*Yield: 16 servings*

# Fresh Blueberry Squares

This cake is like a giant blueberry muffin — the kind that's light, sweet, and filled with lots of luscious berries. It makes a wonderful casual summer dessert, especially when accompanied by ice cream, frozen yogurt, or sorbet. It's also ideal to serve at brunch.

*Note:* This cake should be stored in the refrigerator.

## TOPPING

- 1/4 **cup sugar**
- 2 **tablespoons flour**
- 1/2 **stick (4 tablespoons) butter or margarine, softened**
- 1 **teaspoon cinnamon**

## CAKE

- 3 **eggs**
- 1 **cup sugar**
- 2 **sticks (1 cup) butter or margarine, melted**
- 1 **tablespoon vanilla**
- 1 **cup buttermilk or 1 tablespoon vinegar in a measuring cup plus milk up to the 1-cup mark**
- 2 3/4 **cups flour**
- 1 **tablespoon baking powder**
- 1/8 **teaspoon salt**
- 3 **cups blueberries, rinsed and dried**

1. To make the topping, in a small bowl, using your fingertips, mix together all the topping ingredients until crumbly. Set aside.
2. Preheat the oven to 350°F.
3. Grease and flour a 9" x 13" baking pan.
4. To make the cake, in a large bowl, beat the eggs. Gradually beat in the sugar until the mixture is thick and pale yellow. Beat in the melted butter or margarine, then the vanilla and buttermilk.
5. In another bowl, stir together the flour, baking powder, and salt. Add to the egg mixture, stirring until the dry ingredients are incorporated.
6. Spread the batter in the prepared pan. Sprinkle the blueberries over the batter. Sprinkle the topping over the berries.
7. Bake the cake for 1 hour or until a toothpick inserted in the center comes out clean. Transfer the pan to a rack to cool.

*Preparation time: 25 minutes*
*Yield: 20 servings*

# Peach and Plum Cake

This cake, similar to a pineapple upside-down cake, uses fresh peach and plum slices to impart a wonderful fruity favor The cake is delicious warm from the oven with a dollop of whipped cream. It's also a good choice for Sunday brunch.

*Note:* This cake should be stored in the refrigerator.

## TOPPING
        2   tablespoons butter or margarine
        1/4   cup sugar
        2   plums, pitted and thinly sliced
        1   large peach, peeled, stoned, and
               thinly sliced

## CAKE
        1 1/2   sticks (3/4 cup) butter or margarine,
               softened
        1   cup sugar
        2   eggs
        2/3   cup milk
        1/4   cup brandy
        2   teaspoons vanilla
        2   cups flour
        2   teaspoons baking powder
        1/4   teaspoon salt

1. To make the topping, in a deep, ovenproof skillet (about 9" in diameter), melt the butter

or margarine. Add the sugar, and cook, stirring, until bubbly. Remove the pan from the heat, and arrange the peach and plum slices on the bottom. Set aside.

2. Preheat the oven to 350°F.
3. To make the cake, in a large bowl, cream the butter or margarine with the sugar until the sugar is fully incorporated. Beat in the eggs, then the milk, brandy, and vanilla.
4. In another bowl, stir together the flour, baking powder, and salt. Add to the creamed mixture, stirring until the dry ingredients are incorporated.
5. Carefully pour the batter over the fruit in the skillet. Bake the cake for 45 minutes or until a toothpick inserted in the center comes out clean.
6. Very carefully, turn the cake upside down over a large, round ovenproof platter. If any of the topping has stuck to the skillet, use a knife to spread it over the top of the cake. Return the cake to the oven for 5 minutes to bake the topping. Place the platter on a rack to cool.

*Preparation time: 30 minutes*
*Yield: 10 to 12 servings*

# Strawberry-Rhubarb Coffee Cake

One of the harbingers of spring, rhubarb has a tart flavor that, in this cake, is complemented by fresh strawberries. The hearty, not-too-sweet coffee cake contains a ribbon of fruit through the center and a cinnamon-spiced streusel topping.

*Note:* This cake should be stored in the refrigerator. For best flavor, bring it to room temperature before serving it.

## FILLING
- 1   cup diced rhubarb
- 1   cup thickly sliced strawberries
- $1/3$   cup sugar
- 2   tablespoons cornstarch

## STREUSEL
- $1/3$   cup flour
- 2   tablespoons sugar
- $1/2$   teaspoon cinnamon
- 2   tablespoons butter or margarine, softened

## CAKE
- 10   tablespoons butter or margarine, softened
- $3/4$   cup sugar
- 1   egg
- $3/4$   cup buttermilk or 2 teaspoons vinegar in a measuring cup plus milk up to the $3/4$-cup mark

1 teaspoon vanilla
1 tablespoon grated orange peel
1 cup flour
1 cup whole-wheat flour
1 teaspoon baking powder
$1/2$ teaspoon baking soda
$1/2$ teaspoon cinnamon
$1/8$ teaspoon salt

1. To make the filling, in a medium saucepan, place all the filling ingredients. Cook over a low heat, stirring quite often, until the fruit is softened and the filling thickens, about 10 minutes. Set aside.
2. To make the streusel, in a small bowl, mix all the streusel ingredients until crumbly. Set aside.
3. Preheat the oven to 350°F.
4. Grease and flour a 9" square baking pan.
5. To make the cake, in a large bowl, cream the butter or margarine with the sugar until the sugar is fully incorporated. Beat in the egg, then the buttermilk, vanilla, and orange peel.
6. In another bowl, stir together the flour, whole-wheat flour, baking powder, baking soda, cinnamon, and salt. Add to the creamed mixture, stirring until the dry ingredients are incorporated.
7. Spread about two-thirds of the batter on the bottom and a little up the sides of the prepared pan. Spread the filling evenly over the batter. Drop the remaining batter by spoonfuls over

the filling. With a knife, spread to make even. (The batter will not cover the filling completely.) Sprinkle the streusel mixture over the top.

8. Bake the cake for 50 minutes or until a toothpick inserted in the center comes out clean. Transfer the pan to a rack to cool.

*Preparation time: 30 minutes*
*Yield: 12 servings*

# Mediterranean Orange Cake

Flavors of Mediterranean cuisines — orange, almond, honey, and Madeira — combine in this lovely cake. The syrup poured over the baked cake helps keep it fresh for days.

## CAKE

- ¾ cup raisins
- ¼ cup Madeira
- 1 stick (½ cup) butter or margarine, softened
- 1 cup sugar
- 3 eggs
- 1½ teaspoons grated orange rind
- 1 teaspoon vanilla
- ½ cup orange juice
- 2 cups minus 2 tablespoons flour
- 2 teaspoons baking powder
- ¼ teaspoon salt
- ¼ cup chopped almonds

## SYRUP

- ¼ cup honey
- 1 tablespoon orange juice

1. In a small bowl, mix the raisins and Madeira. Set aside.
2. Preheat the oven to 350°F.
3. Grease and flour a tube pan.
4. To make the cake, in a large bowl, cream the

butter or margarine with the sugar until the sugar is fully incorporated. Beat in the eggs, then the orange rind, vanilla, and orange juice.

5. In another bowl, stir together the flour, baking powder, and salt. Add to the creamed mixture, stirring until the dry ingredients are incorporated. Stir in the almonds, raisins, and any Madeira that wasn't absorbed.

6. Turn the batter out into the prepared pan. Bake the cake for 50 minutes or until a toothpick inserted in the highest part of the cake comes out clean.

7. To make the syrup, while the cake is baking, heat the honey and orange juice in a small saucepan just until they come to a simmer. Spoon this mixture over the cake as soon as it comes from the oven. Transfer the pan to a rack to cool.

*Preparation time: 25 minutes*
*Yield: 10 servings*

# Marbled Cranberry Cake

A simple white cake is marbled with a swirl of honeyed cranberries in this wonderful fall dessert that's perfect for people who enjoy this tart, tangy fruit. Lemon–Cream Cheese Icing (page 338) complements the flavors of the cake.

|  |  |
|---|---|
| 1 | 12-ounce package (3 cups) cranberries, rinsed |
| 3/4 | cup honey |
| 1 | stick (1/2 cup) butter or margarine, softened |
| 1 1/2 | cups sugar |
| 3 | eggs |
| 1 | cup milk |
| 1/2 | teaspoon almond extract |
| 2 1/3 | cups flour |
| 1 | tablespoon baking powder |
| 1/4 | teaspoon salt |

1. Place the cranberries and honey in a medium-size saucepan. Bring to a simmer. Cook over a fairly low heat, uncovered, until the cranberries pop and the mixture thickens, about 10 minutes. Remove from the heat.
2. Preheat the oven to 375°F.
3. Grease and flour a 9" X 13" baking pan.
4. In a large bowl, cream the butter or margarine with the sugar until the sugar is fully incorporated. Beat in the eggs, then the milk and

almond extract.

5. In another bowl, stir together the flour, baking powder, and salt. Add to the creamed mixture, stirring until the dry ingredients are incorporated.

6. Spread the batter evenly in the prepared pan. Pour the cranberry mixture over the top. Using a knife, swirl the cranberry mixture through the batter to create a marbleized effect.

7. Bake the cake for 45 minutes or until a toothpick inserted in the center comes out clean. Transfer the pan to a rack to cool.

*Preparation time: 30 minutes*
*Yield: 15 servings*

# Cranberry Butter Cake

This is a buttery-rich pound cake that's enhanced with orange peel, fresh cranberries, and walnuts. It's festive enough for a holiday buffet table or makes a lovely gift.

2 sticks (1 cup) butter or margarine, softened (try to use at least half butter)
2 cups sugar
5 eggs
¼ cup milk
¼ cup orange juice
1 teaspoon grated orange rind
2 teaspoons vanilla
2¼ cups flour
1 teaspoon baking powder
¼ teaspoon salt
1½ cups cranberries
1 cup chopped walnuts

1. Preheat the oven to 350°F.
2. Grease and flour a tube pan.
3. In a large bowl, cream the butter or margarine with the sugar until the sugar is fully incorporated. Beat in the eggs, then the milk, orange juice, orange rind, and vanilla.
4. In another bowl, stir together the flour, baking powder, and salt. Add to the creamed mixture, stirring until the dry ingredients are incorpo-

rated. Stir in the cranberries and walnuts.

5. Turn the batter out into the prepared pan. Bake the cake for 1 hour 20 minutes or until a toothpick inserted in the highest part of the cake comes out clean. Transfer the pan to a rack to cool.

*Preparation time: 20 minutes*
*Yield: 14 to 16 servings*

# Cranberry-Peach Upside-Down Cake

From the number of cranberry recipes in this book, it shouldn't come as a surprise that these berries are among my favorite fruits for baking. For one thing, there's virtually no preparation required — just open a bag and rinse. They are also pleasingly tart, which provides a good counterpoint to sweet cake. Finally, cranberries are very attractive, and nowhere is this more apparent than in this upside-down ginger cake that shows off their bright red color in lovely contrast to golden peaches.

*Note:* If you prefer to use fresh fruit rather than canned and cannot find peaches, you may substitute pears. Choose 3 to 4 pears that have ripened completely; peel, halve, and core them. This cake should be stored in the refrigerator.

## TOPPING
- ½ stick (4 tablespoons) butter or margarine
- ½ cup brown sugar, preferably dark
- 6 to 8 canned peach halves
- 1 cup cranberries

## CAKE
- 9 tablespoons butter or margarine, softened
- ¾ cup sugar
- 2 eggs
- ½ cup milk
- 1½ cups flour

1 **teaspoon baking powder**
1 **teaspoon ginger**

1. To make the topping, in a heavy, ovenproof 9" skillet, melt the butter or margarine. Stir in the brown sugar. Remove from the heat. Place the peach halves, cut side up, in an attractive pattern in the skillet, and scatter the cranberries over all. Set aside.
2. Preheat the oven to 350°F.
3. To make the cake, in a large bowl, cream the butter or margarine with the sugar until the sugar is fully incorporated. Beat in the eggs, then the milk.
4. In another bowl, stir together the flour, baking powder, and ginger. Add to the creamed mixture, stirring until the dry ingredients are incorporated.
5. Pour the batter carefully over the fruit in the skillet. Bake the cake for 50 minutes or until a toothpick inserted in the center comes out clean.
6. Very carefully tip the cake out onto an ovenproof platter, so that the fruit is now on top. With a knife, spread on any topping that has adhered to the skillet. Return the cake to the oven for 5 to 10 minutes or until the topping is set. Transfer the platter to a rack to cool.

*Preparation time: 30 minutes*
*Yield: 10 to 12 servings*

# Mincemeat-Cranberry Pound Cake

If you've only tasted mincemeat as a thick, gooey pie filling, I want you to know that this ingredient becomes transformed when baked into a cake. Mincemeat contributes to the cake's lovely texture, while the spices, apples, and raisins in it add a wonderful flavor — all with remarkably little work on the part of the baker. And the tangy cranberries complement the sweet mincemeat perfectly. This is a large attractive cake that's perfect for holiday gatherings.

   2  **sticks (1 cup) butter or margarine, softened (try to use at least half butter)**
   2  **cups sugar**
   6  **eggs**
   ½  **cup milk**
   1  **tablespoon vanilla**
   1  **27-ounce jar prepared mincemeat pie filling**
   3  **cups flour**
   2  **teaspoons baking powder**
  1½  **cups cranberries, coarsely chopped**

1. Preheat the oven to 325°F.
2. Grease and flour a tube pan.
3. In a large bowl, cream the butter or margarine with the sugar until the sugar is fully incorpo-

rated. Beat in the eggs very well, then the milk and vanilla, followed by the mincemeat.

4. In another bowl, stir together the flour and baking powder. Add to the mincemeat mixture, stirring just until the dry ingredients are incorporated. Stir in the cranberries.

5. Turn the batter out into the prepared pan. Bake the cake for 2¾ hours or until a toothpick inserted in the highest part of the cake comes out clean. Transfer the pan to a rack to cool.

*Preparation time: 25 minutes*
*Yield: 20 to 25 servings*

# Cranberry Streusel Cake

Sour cream coffee cakes filled with streusel are among my favorite cakes. This one's enhanced with flavorful, tangy dried cranberries. It's a great cake for brunch as well as for snacking.

**STREUSEL**
- ¼ cup brown sugar, preferably dark
- 1 tablespoon flour
- 1 tablespoon butter or margarine, softened
- 1½ teaspoons cinnamon
- ¼ teaspoon nutmeg

**CAKE**
- 1½ sticks (¾ cup) butter or margarine, softened
- 1½ cups sugar
- 4 eggs
- 1 cup sour cream
- ¼ cup milk
- 1 teaspoon vanilla
- ½ teaspoon almond extract
- 3 cups flour
- 1½ teaspoons baking powder
- ½ teaspoon baking soda
- ¼ teaspoon salt
- 1 cup dried cranberries

1. To make the streusel, in a small bowl, mix together the streusel ingredients using your fingertips, until the mixture is crumbly. Set aside.
2. Preheat the oven to 350°F.
3. Grease and flour a tube pan.
4. To make the cake, in a large bowl, cream the butter or margarine with the sugar until the sugar is fully incorporated. Beat in the eggs, then the sour cream, milk, vanilla, and almond extract.
5. In another bowl, stir together the flour, baking powder, baking soda, and salt. Add to the creamed mixture, stirring just until the dry ingredients are incorporated. Stir in the cranberries.
6. Spread half the batter evenly in the prepared pan. Sprinkle with the streusel. Add the remaining batter. Bake the cake for 1 hour 20 minutes or until a toothpick inserted in the highest part of the cake comes out clean. Transfer the pan to a rack to cool.

*Preparation time: 25 minutes*
*Yield: 18 to 20 servings*

# Apple-Apricot Fruitcake

When people say they don't like fruitcake, what they usually mean is that they don't enjoy eating those gummy candied fruits available in the supermarket for holiday baking. While high-quality glacéed fruits can be difficult to track down, a fruitcake made with dried fruits, which are easily obtained, is just as festive as traditional fruitcake but with a wonderful flavor and texture. This one mixes walnuts, almonds, dark and golden raisins, dried apricots, and apple for a truly memorable taste experience.

- 2 sticks (1 cup) butter or margarine, softened
- 1 cup brown sugar, preferably dark
- 3 eggs
- ²/₃ cup applesauce
- 1 medium apple, peeled, cored, and grated (about ²/₃ cup)
- ¹/₂ cup brandy
- ¹/₃ cup apple juice
- 1¹/₂ teaspoons vanilla
- 1¹/₃ cups flour
- 1 cup whole-wheat flour
- 1 teaspoon baking powder
- ¹/₄ teaspoon baking soda
- ¹/₄ teaspoon salt
- ³/₄ teaspoon cinnamon
- ³/₄ teaspoon nutmeg
- 1¹/₃ cups chopped walnuts

1⅓ cups chopped almonds
⅔ cup dark raisins
1 cup golden raisins
6 ounces dried apricots, coarsely chopped (about 1½ cups)

1. Preheat the oven to 325°F.
2. Grease and flour a tube pan.
3. In a large bowl, cream the butter or margarine with the sugar until the sugar is fully incorporated. Beat in the eggs, then the applesauce, grated apple, brandy, apple juice, and vanilla.
4. In another bowl, stir together the flour, whole-wheat flour, baking powder, baking soda, salt, cinnamon, and nutmeg. Add to the creamed mixture, stirring until the dry ingredients are incorporated. Stir in the walnuts, almonds, dark raisins, golden raisins, and apricots.
5. Spread the batter evenly in the prepared pan. Bake the cake for 1½ hours or until a toothpick inserted in the highest part of the cake comes out clean. Transfer the pan to a rack to cool.

*Preparation time: 30 minutes*
*Yield: 20 servings*

# Mixed-Fruit Butter Cake

This rich butter cake is topped with dried fruits that have been simmered in orange juice and port. Like a sophisticated version of pineapple upside-down cake, it is delicious warm from the oven, topped with a scoop of vanilla ice cream or frozen yogurt.

## TOPPING
- 1 8-ounce package mixed dried fruits, coarsely chopped
- $1/3$ cup raisins
- $1/2$ cup orange juice
- $1/4$ cup port
- 3 tablespoons butter or margarine
- 2 teaspoons vanilla
- $1/3$ cup sugar

## CAKE
- 2 sticks (1 cup) butter or margarine, softened (try to use at least half butter)
- 1 cup sugar
- 2 eggs
- $1/3$ cup milk
- 2 teaspoons vanilla
- 2 cups flour
- 1 teaspoon baking powder
- $1/4$ teaspoon baking soda
- $1/8$ teaspoon salt

1. To make the topping, in a small saucepan, combine the mixed fruits, raisins, orange juice, port, and butter or margarine. Bring to a boil. Lower the heat, and simmer, uncovered, until thick, about 10 minutes. Remove from the heat and add the vanilla. Set aside. (The sugar will be used later.)
2. Preheat the oven to 350°F.
3. Grease and flour a 9" x 13" baking pan.
4. To make the cake, in a large bowl, cream the butter or margarine with the 1 cup of sugar until the sugar is fully incorporated. Beat in the eggs, then the milk and vanilla.
5. In another bowl, stir together the flour, baking powder, baking soda, and salt. Add to the creamed mixture, stirring until the dry ingredients are incorporated.
6. Turn the batter out into the prepared pan. Spread the topping evenly over the batter, and sprinkle with the $1/3$ cup of sugar. Bake the cake for 40 minutes or until a toothpick inserted in the center comes out clean. Transfer the pan to a rack to cool.

*Preparation time: 30 minutes*
*Yield: 14 to 16 servings*

# Chip 'n' Nut Date Cake

Water softens the dates in this cake and intensifies the date flavor in the batter. Chocolate chips and pecans enhance the cake without overpowering the delicate taste of the dates. This cakes stays fresh for days.

| | |
|---|---|
| 1¼ | cups boiling water |
| 4 | ounces (¾ cup) chopped dates |
| 1½ | sticks (¾ cup) butter or margarine, softened |
| 1 | cup sugar |
| 2 | eggs |
| 1 | teaspoon vanilla |
| ¾ | cup flour |
| ¾ | cup whole-wheat flour |
| 2 | teaspoons baking powder |
| 1 | teaspoon cinnamon |
| ¼ | teaspoon salt |
| ½ | cup finely chopped semisweet chocolate or chocolate morsels |
| ¾ | cup pecans |

1. In a small bowl, pour the boiling water over the dates. Let sit until lukewarm.
2. Preheat the oven to 350°F.
3. Grease and flour a tube pan.
4. In a large bowl, cream the butter or margarine with the sugar until the sugar is fully incorporated. Beat in the eggs, then the vanilla and

dates plus the water.

5. In another bowl, stir together the flour, whole-wheat flour, baking powder, cinnamon, and salt. Add to the date mixture, stirring until the dry ingredients are incorporated. Stir in the chocolate and pecans.

6. Turn the batter out into the prepared pan. Bake the cake for 55 minutes or until a tooth-pick inserted in the highest part of the cake comes out clean. Transfer the pan to a rack to cool.

*Preparation time: 25 minutes*
*Yield: 12 to 14 servings*

# Spiced Date Cake

Reminiscent of date-nut breads, this is delicious warm from the oven and cut into large squares. If you have the willpower to wait before eating it, Caramel Icing (page 336) makes a great topping for this cake.

2    sticks (1 cup) butter or margarine, softened
$^3/_4$  cup sugar
$^2/_3$  cup molasses
2    eggs
$^3/_4$  cup buttermilk or 2 teaspoons vinegar in a measuring cup plus milk up to the $^3/_4$-cup mark
     Grated rind 1 orange
$1^1/_4$ cups flour
1    cup whole-wheat flour
$2^1/_2$ teaspoons baking powder
$^1/_2$  teaspoon baking soda
1    teaspoon cinnamon
$^1/_2$  teaspoon ground cloves
$^1/_4$  teaspoon salt
$^3/_4$  cup chopped dates
$^3/_4$  cup chopped walnuts

1. Preheat the oven to 350°F.
2. Grease and flour a 9" X 13" baking pan.
3. In a large bowl, cream the butter or margarine with the sugar and molasses until the sugar is

fully incorporated. Beat in the eggs, then the buttermilk and orange rind.

4. In another bowl, stir together the flour, whole-wheat flour, baking powder, baking soda, cinnamon, cloves, and salt. Add to the creamed mixture, stirring until the dry ingredients are incorporated. Stir in the dates and walnuts.

5. Spread the batter evenly in the prepared pan. Bake the cake for 40 minutes or until a toothpick inserted in the center comes out clean. Transfer the pan to a rack to cool.

*Preparation time: 25 minutes*
*Yield: 16 to 18 servings*

# Sour Cream–Fig Cake

Chopped dried figs and crunchy walnuts lend texture and flavor to this sour cream butter cake. It is an especially easy cake to make and keeps well for days.

|       |                                              |
|-------|----------------------------------------------|
| 2     | sticks (1 cup) butter or margarine, softened |
| 1½    | cups sugar                                   |
| 4     | eggs                                         |
| 1     | cup sour cream                               |
| ⅓     | cup milk                                     |
| ⅓     | cup brandy                                   |
| 2     | teaspoons vanilla                            |
| 3     | cups flour                                   |
| 1     | tablespoon baking powder                     |
| ½     | teaspoon nutmeg                              |
| ½     | teaspoon baking soda                         |
| ¼     | teaspoon salt                                |
| 1½    | cups chopped dried figs                      |
| 1     | cup chopped walnuts                          |

1. Preheat the oven to 325°F.
2. Grease and flour a tube pan.
3. In a large bowl, cream the butter or margarine with the sugar until the sugar is fully incorporated. Beat in the eggs, then the sour cream, milk, brandy, and vanilla.
4. In another bowl, stir together the flour, baking powder, nutmeg, baking soda, and salt. Add

to the creamed mixture, stirring until the dry ingredients are incorporated. Stir in the figs and walnuts.

5. Spread the batter evenly in the prepared pan. Bake the cake for 1½ hours or until a toothpick inserted in the highest part of the cake comes out clean. Transfer the pan to a rack to cool.

*Preparation time: 25 minutes*
*Yield: 18 to 20 servings*

# Chocolate-Pecan-Raisin Cake

This recipe combines three favorite cakes — a classic buttery raisin pound cake, a deep, dark chocolate cake, and a mellow pecan cake — into a single wonderful creation. To enhance the chocolate flavor, cover the cake with Chocolate Butter Frosting (page 339).

| | |
|---:|---|
| 2 | **sticks (1 cup) butter or margarine, softened** |
| 1¼ | **cups sugar** |
| 3 | **eggs** |
| ¼ | **cup dry sherry** |
| 1 | **cup water** |
| 1 | **teaspoon vanilla** |
| 2¼ | **cups flour** |
| ¾ | **cup unsweetened cocoa powder, sifted if lumpy** |
| 1 | **teaspoon baking soda** |
| ½ | **teaspoon baking powder** |
| ¼ | **teaspoon salt** |
| 1 | **cup dark raisins** |
| 1 | **cup golden raisins** |
| 2 | **cups chopped pecans** |

1. Preheat the oven to 300°F.
2. Grease and flour a tube pan.
3. In a large bowl, cream the butter or margarine with the sugar until the sugar is fully incorporated. Beat in the eggs, then the sherry, water,

and vanilla.

4. In another bowl, stir together the flour, cocoa, baking soda, baking powder, and salt. Add to the creamed mixture, stirring until the dry ingredients are incorporated. Stir in the dark raisins, golden raisins, and pecans.

5. Spread the batter evenly in the prepared pan. Bake the cake 1¾ to 2 hours or until a toothpick inserted in the highest part of the cake comes out clean. Transfer the pan to a rack to cool.

*Preparation time: 25 minutes*
*Yield: 16 to 18 servings*

# Dried-Pineapple Cake

Sweet chunks of dried pineapple lend a distinctive flavor to this buttery spice cake. Since the cake keeps fresh for days, it is an excellent choice for shipping.

- 2 cups boiling water
- 8 ounces dried pineapple, diced
- 2 sticks (1 cup) butter or margarine, melted
- 1 cup sugar
- 4 eggs
- ½ cup heavy cream or whipping cream
- 2 cups flour
- 1 cup whole-wheat flour
- 1 tablespoon baking powder
- 1 teaspoon cinnamon
- ½ teaspoon nutmeg
- ¼ teaspoon ginger
- ¼ teaspoon ground cloves
- ¼ teaspoon salt
- 1 cup chopped pecans

1. In a bowl, pour the boiling water over the pineapple. Set aside.
2. Preheat the oven to 350°F.
3. Grease and flour a tube pan.
4. In a large bowl, cream the butter or margarine with the sugar until the sugar is fully incorporated. Beat in the eggs, then the cream.

5. In another bowl, stir together the flour, whole-wheat flour, baking powder, cinnamon, nutmeg, ginger, cloves, and salt. Add to the creamed mixture, stirring until the dry ingredients are incorporated. Drain the pineapple well, discarding the water, and add it to the batter along with the pecans.
6. Spread the batter evenly in the prepared pan. Bake the cake for 1 hour 15 minutes or until a toothpick inserted in the highest part of the cake comes out clean. Transfer the pan to a rack to cool.

*Preparation time: 25 minutes*
*Yield: 20 servings*

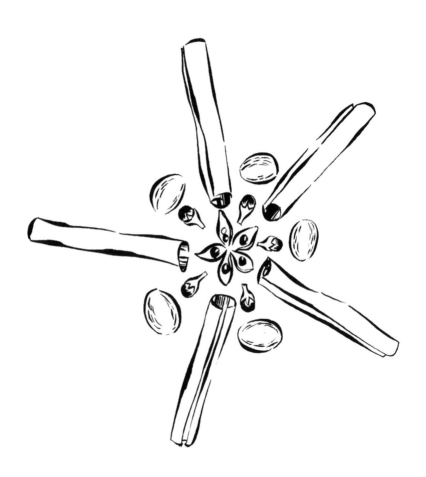

# CHAPTER FOUR

# SPICE CAKES

Spices — especially cinnamon, nutmeg, ginger, and cloves — add so much taste and fragrance to cakes that they are used frequently in all the chapters of this book. Chapter 4 is devoted to those cakes that are so heady with spices, there can be no question about what category of cake they belong to. Spice cakes are among the most quickly put-together of all cakes, for the entire batter is flavored in just the few seconds it takes to measure out cinnamon or nutmeg. And the rewards of such cakes are not only in the eating, but also in the marvelous perfume that they release during baking.

# Guinness Spice Cake

When ale or beer is used in baking, it imparts a dark color and light texture — qualities that are accentuated by the addition of Guinness stout, which is thick and dark. Molasses, plenty of spices, and an assortment of dried fruits contribute to making this an extraordinarily flavorful spice cake that stays fresh for days.

- 2 sticks (1 cup) butter or margarine, softened
- 1 cup brown sugar, preferably dark
- 1/3 cup molasses
- 3 eggs
  Grated rind 1 orange
  Grated rind 1 lemon
- 1/2 cup Guinness stout, at room temperature, plus another 1/3 cup to pour over the cake
- 3 1/4 cups flour
- 1 teaspoon baking soda
- 1 teaspoon cinnamon
- 1 teaspoon nutmeg
- 1 teaspoon cardamom
- 1/4 teaspoon ground cloves
- 1/4 teaspoon salt
- 1/2 cup chopped dates
- 1/2 cup chopped prunes
- 1/2 cup raisins
- 3/4 cup chopped walnuts

1. Preheat the oven to 325°F.
2. Grease and flour a tube pan.
3. In a large bowl, cream the butter or margarine with the sugar and molasses until the sugar is fully incorporated. Beat in the eggs, then the orange rind, lemon rind, and the ½ cup of stout.
4. In another bowl, stir together the flour, baking soda, cinnamon, nutmeg, cardamom, cloves, and salt. Add to the creamed mixture, stirring until the dry ingredients are incorporated. Stir in the dates, prunes, raisins, and walnuts.
5. Turn the batter out into the prepared pan. Bake the cake for 1½ hours or until a toothpick inserted in the highest part of the cake comes out clean. Prick the top of the cake several times with a fork, and pour the ⅓ cup of stout over it. Transfer the pan to a rack to cool.

*Preparation time: 30 minutes*
*Yield: 20 to 24 servings*

# Cocoa Spice Cake

Spice cakes often call for a small amount of cocoa to enhance the flavor of the spices. But this cake contains so much cocoa, it practically shares equal billing with the spices. The result is a dark, chocolaty spice cake. Caramel Icing (page 336) plays up the flavor of the brown sugar in the cake and adds to its sweetness.

2 sticks (1 cup) butter or margarine, softened
1½ cups sugar
1½ cups brown sugar, preferably dark
4 eggs
1¾ cups milk
1½ teaspoons vanilla
3 cups flour
⅔ cup unsweetened cocoa powder, sifted if lumpy
4½ teaspoons baking powder
1½ teaspoons cinnamon
¾ teaspoon nutmeg
¼ teaspoon ground cloves
¼ teaspoon salt

1. Preheat the oven to 350°F.
2. Grease and flour a 9" x 13" baking pan.
3. In a large bowl, cream the butter or margarine with the sugar and brown sugar until the sugars are fully incorporated. Beat in the eggs,

then the milk and vanilla.

4. In another bowl, stir together the flour, cocoa, baking powder, cinnamon, nutmeg, cloves, and salt. Add to the creamed mixture, stirring until the dry ingredients are incorporated.
5. Turn the batter out into the prepared pan. Bake the cake for 1 hour or until a toothpick inserted in the center comes out clean. Transfer the pan to a rack to cool.

*Preparation time: 20 minutes*
*Yield: 20 servings*

# Spiced Carrot Cake

Carrot cakes have become increasingly popular over the past couple of decades. This is because, rather than tasting like a vegetable, grated carrots contribute a crunchy texture. Raisins, walnuts, and chocolate chips make this carrot cake especially delectable. Creamy White Icing (page 334) turns the cake into a "party" dessert.

4 eggs
³/₄ cup sugar, preferably dark brown
2 sticks (1 cup) butter or margarine, melted
¹/₂ cup orange juice
2 cups flour
2 teaspoons baking powder
2 teaspoons cinnamon
¹/₂ teaspoon nutmeg
3 medium carrots, peeled and grated (about 1¹/₂ cups)
²/₃ cup semisweet mini-chocolate morsels
¹/₂ cup raisins
¹/₂ cup chopped walnuts

1. Preheat the oven to 350°F.
2. Grease and flour a tube pan.
3. In a large bowl, beat the eggs. Gradually beat in the sugar until the mixture is thick. Beat in the melted butter or margarine, then the or-

ange juice.

4. In another bowl, stir together the flour, baking powder, cinnamon, and nutmeg. Add to the egg mixture, stirring until the dry ingredients are incorporated. Stir in the carrots, chocolate, raisins, and walnuts.

5. Turn the batter out into the prepared pan. Bake the cake for 1 hour or until a toothpick inserted in the highest part of the cake comes out clean. Transfer the pan to a rack to cool.

*Preparation time: 30 minutes*
*Yield: 12 to 14 servings*

# Nut-Topped Gingerbread

Honey combines with molasses to make this gingerbread more mellow than most. The broiled-on nut topping is deliciously sweet and crunchy. This gingerbread may be served warm from the oven or at room temperature.

## CAKE
1   **stick ($\frac{1}{2}$ cup) butter or margarine, softened**
1   **cup sugar**
$\frac{1}{2}$   **cup honey**
$\frac{1}{2}$   **cup molasses**
2   **eggs**
1   **cup buttermilk or 1 tablespoon vinegar in a measuring cup plus milk up to the 1-cup mark**
$1\frac{1}{2}$   **cups flour**
$1\frac{1}{2}$   **cups whole-wheat flour**
1   **teaspoon baking soda**
2   **teaspoons ginger**
2   **teaspoons cinnamon**
1   **teaspoon nutmeg**
$\frac{1}{4}$   **teaspoon ground cloves**

## TOPPING
$\frac{3}{4}$   **stick (6 tablespoons) butter or margarine**
$\frac{1}{3}$   **cup sugar**
2   **tablespoons flour**
2   **tablespoons milk**

**2 cups chopped walnuts**

1. Preheat the oven to 350°F.
2. Grease and flour a 9" X 13" baking pan.
3. To make the cake, in a large bowl, cream the butter or margarine with the sugar, honey, and molasses until the sugar is completely incorporated. Beat in the eggs, then the buttermilk.
4. In another bowl, stir together the flour, whole-wheat flour, baking soda, ginger, cinnamon, nutmeg, and cloves. Add to the creamed mixture, stirring until the dry ingredients are incorporated.
5. Spread the batter evenly in the prepared pan. Bake the cake for 45 minutes or until a toothpick inserted in the center comes out clean.
6. To make the topping while the cake is baking, in a saucepan, combine all the topping ingredients. Bring to a boil, stirring occasionally. Remove the pan from the heat.
7. As soon as the cake is done baking, gently spread the topping over it. Broil the cake about 3" from the heat source until bubbly, about 1 minute. Transfer the pan to a rack to cool.

*Preparation time: 30 minutes*
*Yield: 20 servings*

# Gingersnap Gingerbread

A mixture of gingersnap crumbs, pecans, and brown sugar makes this gingerbread deliciously special. Serve it warm from the oven or at room temperature. If you wish to gild the lily, spread the completely cooled cake with Lemon–Cream Cheese Icing (page 338).

## GINGERSNAP MIXTURE

- 1 cup finely chopped pecans
- 1 cup (about 30 1" cookies) finely crushed gingersnaps
- $1/2$ cup brown sugar, preferably dark
- $1/2$ stick (4 tablespoons) butter or margarine, melted

## CAKE

- 6 tablespoons butter or margarine, softened
- $1/3$ cup sugar
- $3/4$ cup molasses
- 2 eggs
- $2/3$ cup buttermilk or 2 teaspoons vinegar in a measuring cup plus milk up to the $2/3$-cup mark
- 1 cup flour
- $3/4$ cup whole-wheat flour
- 1 teaspoon ginger
- 1 teaspoon cinnamon
- 1 teaspoon baking soda
- $1/8$ teaspoon salt

1. To make the gingersnap mixture, mix together the gingersnap-mixture ingredients. Set aside.
2. Preheat the oven to 350°F.
3. Grease and flour an 8" x 10" baking pan.
4. To make the cake, in a large bowl, cream the butter or margarine with the sugar and molasses until the sugar is fully incorporated. Beat in the eggs, then the buttermilk.
5. In another bowl, stir together the flour, whole-wheat flour, ginger, cinnamon, baking soda, and salt. Add to the creamed mixture, stirring until the dry ingredients are incorporated.
6. Sprinkle half the gingersnap mixture over the bottom of the prepared pan. Spread evenly with half the cake batter. Repeat.
7. Bake the cake for 45 minutes or until a toothpick inserted in the center comes out clean. Transfer the pan to a rack to cool.

*Preparation time: 25 minutes*
*Yield: 12 servings*

# Mellow Maple Cake

This is an example of a perfect spice cake. The buttermilk makes for a light texture, the mixture of spices lingers on the palate, and the maple syrup adds a subtle flavor of its own. Mellow Maple Cake is an ideal choice for potluck suppers or picnics and also travels well in a child's lunchbox.

   1   stick (½ cup) butter or margarine, softened
   1   cup maple syrup (*not* imitation maple flavoring)
 1½   cups sugar
   3   eggs
 1½   cups buttermilk or 4 teaspoons vinegar in a measuring cup plus milk up to the 1½-cup mark
 1½   cups flour
 1½   cups whole-wheat flour
   1   tablespoon cinnamon
   1   teaspoon ginger
   1   teaspoon nutmeg
   1   teaspoon baking soda
   1   teaspoon baking powder
   ¼   teaspoon salt


1. Preheat the oven to 350°F.
2. Grease and flour a tube pan.
3. In a large bowl, cream the butter or margarine

with the maple syrup and sugar until the sugar is fully incorporated. Beat in the eggs, then the buttermilk.

4. In another bowl, stir together the flour, whole-wheat flour, cinnamon, ginger, nutmeg, baking soda, baking powder, and salt. Add to the creamed mixture, stirring until the dry ingredients are incorporated.

5. Turn the batter out into the prepared pan. Bake 1 hour 20 minutes or until a toothpick inserted in the highest part of the cake comes out clean. Transfer the pan to a rack to cool.

*Preparation time: 20 minutes*
*Yield: 20 servings*

# Saffron-Raisin Pound Cake

I watched a chef on TV prepare a saffron-flavored flan. As he spoke of the wonderful taste saffron imparts to desserts, I realized I couldn't even identify the flavor of this spice. Since I had sampled saffron only in savory dishes like paella, I always associated it with seafood, never with desserts. So I developed a cake to see how saffron tastes in desserts. This pound cake is sensational. It's difficult to describe saffron's flavor. The best I can do is to say it's subtle. Try it for yourself.

Saffron certainly deserves its reputation as the world's most expensive spice. Although the minuscule vial I purchased set me back only a couple of dollars, I calculated that a pound of saffron would come to about $2,000! Saffron is made from the dried stigmas of a small purple crocus (Crocus sativus). Be sure the saffron you purchase is in threads, not the powdered form, which often is less pure.

*Note:* This cake is even better the day after it has been baked because the saffron favor becomes more pronounced.

0.2 **grams (about ¼ teaspoon) saffron**
⅔ **cup milk**
1 **cup raisins**
2 **sticks (1 cup) butter or margarine, softened (try to use at least half butter)**
2 **cups sugar**
5 **eggs**

158

1 teaspoon vanilla
2¹/₂ cups flour
  2 teaspoons baking powder
  ¹/₄ teaspoon salt


1. Place the saffron and milk in a small saucepan. Heat over medium heat just until the milk reaches the boiling point. (Tiny bubbles will form around the edges of the pan.) Remove the pan from the heat, and stir in the raisins. Let cool slightly.
2. Preheat the oven to 350°F.
3. Grease and flour a tube pan.
4. In a large bowl, cream the butter or margarine with the sugar until the sugar is fully incorporated. Beat in the eggs, then the vanilla. Drain the saffron-milk mixture from the raisins, and beat in. Reserve the raisins.
5. In another bowl, stir together the flour, baking powder, and salt. Add to the creamed mixture, stirring until the dry ingredients are incorporated. Stir in the raisins and any remaining liquid.
6. Turn the batter out into the prepared pan. Bake the cake 1 hour 20 minutes or until a toothpick inserted in the highest part of the cake comes out clean. Transfer the pan to a rack to cool.


*Preparation time: 25 minutes*
*Yield: 16 to 18 servings*

# Hearty Poppy Seed Cake

Most poppy seed cakes are light and delicate. This one, however, is dense and flavorful from the addition of bran cereal, wheat germ, and molasses. The cake has a very pronounced poppy seed flavor, which makes it uniquely satisfying for fans of this ingredient. And it keeps fresh for several days, so it's ideal for shipping.

| | |
|---|---|
| 2 | sticks (1 cup) butter or margarine, softened (try to use at least half butter) |
| $^2/_3$ | cup brown sugar, preferably dark |
| 2 | tablespoons molasses |
| 4 | eggs |
| 1 | $12^1/_2$-ounce can poppy seed filling |
| $^1/_2$ | cup milk |
| 2 | cups flour |
| $^1/_2$ | cup bran cereal such as All-Bran |
| $^1/_4$ | cup wheat germ |
| 2 | teaspoons baking powder |
| $^1/_4$ | teaspoon nutmeg |

1. Preheat the oven to 350°F.
2. Grease and flour a tube pan.
3. In a large bowl, cream the butter or margarine with the brown sugar and molasses until the sugar is fully incorporated. Beat in the eggs, then the poppy seed filling and milk.
4. In another bowl, stir together the flour, bran

160

cereal, wheat germ, baking powder, and nutmeg. Add to the creamed mixture, stirring until the dry ingredients are incorporated.

5. Spread the batter evenly in the prepared pan. Bake the cake for 1 hour 5 minutes or until a toothpick inserted in the highest part of the cake comes out clean. Transfer the pan to a rack to cool.

*Preparation time: 20 minutes*
*Yield: 16 to 18 servings*

# Russian Honey Cake

The addition of sour cream makes this honey cake far richer than most. This is a lovely dessert on its own or accompanied by a fresh fruit salad. To make an especially festive cake, cover it with Creamy White Icing (page 334).

> 3  eggs
> 1  cup brown sugar, preferably dark
> 1  cup honey
> 2  sticks (1 cup) butter or margarine, melted
> 1  cup sour cream
> 1  teaspoon vanilla
> 2½  cups flour
> 1  teaspoon baking powder
> 1  teaspoon baking soda
> 1  teaspoon cinnamon
> ½  teaspoon nutmeg
> ¼  teaspoon ground cloves

1. Preheat the oven to 350°F.
2. Grease and flour a tube pan.
3. In a large bowl, beat the eggs. Gradually, beat in the brown sugar and honey until the mixture is thick. Beat in the melted butter or margarine, then the sour cream and vanilla.
4. In another bowl, stir together the flour, baking powder, baking soda, cinnamon, nutmeg, and cloves. Add to the honey mixture, stirring until

the dry ingredients are incorporated.

5. Turn the batter out into the prepared pan. Bake the cake for 1 hour or until a toothpick inserted in the highest part of the cake comes out clean. Transfer the pan to a rack to cool.

*Preparation time: 20 minutes*
*Yield: 14 to 16 servings*

# Plumped-Raisin Spice Cake

The raisins in this spice cake are plumped and soft, and the cake is wonderfully fragrant. Notice that in this recipe the small amount of cocoa is used as a spice, rather than providing a pronounced chocolate flavor. If you wish to add more than a touch of chocolate, cover the cake with Dark Chocolate Glaze (page 341).

| | |
|---|---|
| 2 | cups raisins |
| 2¹/₂ | cups water |
| 10²/₃ | tablespoons (²/₃ cup) butter or margarine |
| 2 | eggs |
| 1¹/₂ | cups sugar |
| 3¹/₂ | cups flour |
| 2 | teaspoons baking powder |
| 1 | teaspoon baking soda |
| ¹/₄ | cup unsweetened cocoa powder, sifted if lumpy |
| ¹/₂ | teaspoon cinnamon |
| ¹/₂ | teaspoon nutmeg |
| ¹/₄ | teaspoon ground cloves |
| 1 | cup chopped walnuts |

1. In a saucepan, bring the raisins, water, and butter or margarine to a boil. Boil for 1 minute. Remove from the heat, and set aside. Let cool slightly.
2. Preheat the oven to 350°F.

3. Grease and flour a 9" x 13" baking pan.
4. In a large bowl, beat the eggs. Gradually beat in the sugar until the mixture is thick and pale yellow. Drain the liquid from the raisins, and add. Reserve the raisins.
5. In another bowl, stir together the flour, baking powder, baking soda, cocoa, cinnamon, nutmeg, and cloves. Add to the liquid ingredients, stirring until the dry ingredients are incorporated. Stir in the raisins and any remaining liquid, as well as the walnuts.
6. Turn the batter out into the prepared pan. Bake the cake for 45 minutes or until a toothpick inserted in the center comes out clean. Transfer the pan to a rack to cool.

*Preparation time: 25 minutes*
*Yield: 20 servings*

# Orange Syrup Cake

This hearty spice cake is split and drizzled with orange syrup in the middle and over the top. The result is an intensely flavored cake that's fine on its own and even better when accompanied by a scoop of orange sorbet.

## CAKE

1½ sticks (¾ cup) butter or margarine, softened
¾ cup brown sugar, preferably dark
2 eggs
1 tablespoon vanilla
⅔ cup half-and-half or light cream
1 tablespoon vinegar
Grated rind 1 orange
1 cup flour
¾ cup whole-wheat flour
1 teaspoon baking soda
1 teaspoon baking powder
1 teaspoon cinnamon
1 teaspoon nutmeg
¾ teaspoon ground cloves
¼ teaspoon salt
⅔ cup raisins

## SYRUP

½ cup honey
⅔ cup orange juice
Rind 1 orange, removed with a vegetable peeler

1. Preheat the oven to 350°F.
2. Grease and flour a 9" square baking pan.
3. To make the cake, in a large bowl, cream the butter or margarine with the sugar until the sugar is fully incorporated. Beat in the eggs, then the vanilla, half-and-half or light cream, vinegar, and orange rind.
4. In another bowl, stir together the flour, whole-wheat flour, baking soda, baking powder, cinnamon, nutmeg, cloves, and salt. Add to the creamed mixture, stirring until the dry ingredients are incorporated. Stir in the raisins.
5. Turn the batter out into the prepared pan. Bake the cake for 35 minutes or until a toothpick inserted in the center comes out clean. Transfer the pan to a rack to cool.
6. While the cake is cooling, make the syrup. In a small saucepan, stir together the syrup ingredients. Bring to a boil. Lower the heat to a simmer, and cook, uncovered, for 10 minutes. Remove the orange peel.
7. When the cake is completely cool, remove it from the pan, and cut it in half horizontally. Place the bottom half of the cake, cut side up, on a serving plate. Drizzle half the syrup over the cake. Replace the top half of the cake, and drizzle the remaining syrup over the top.

*Preparation time: 30 minutes*
*Yield: 12 servings*

# Nutmeg-Raisin Cake

Although almost all spice cakes contain nutmeg, seldom does this distinctive spice shine on its own. Yet the nuances of nutmeg make it ideal as the single spice in this raisin pound cake. This is an especially easy cake to prepare, and it keeps and ships well.

|   |   |
|--:|---|
| 2 | **cups raisins** |
| ¼ | **cup brandy** |
| 2 | **sticks (1 cup) butter or margarine, softened (try to use at least half butter)** |
| 1¼ | **cups sugar** |
| 5 | **eggs** |
| ¼ | **cup milk** |
| 2¼ | **cups flour** |
| 2½ | **teaspoons nutmeg** |
| 1 | **teaspoon baking powder** |
| ¼ | **teaspoon salt** |
| 1 | **cup chopped walnuts** |

1. In a small bowl, stir together the raisins and brandy. Set aside.
2. Preheat the oven to 325°F.
3. Grease and flour a tube pan.
4. In a large bowl, cream the butter or margarine with the sugar until the sugar is fully incorporated. Beat in the eggs, then the milk.
5. In another bowl, stir together the flour, nut-

meg, baking powder, and salt. Add to the creamed mixture, stirring until the dry ingredients are incorporated. Stir in the walnuts, raisins, and any brandy that wasn't absorbed.

6. Turn the batter out into the prepared pan. Bake the cake for 1 hour or until a toothpick inserted in the highest part of the cake comes out clean. Transfer the pan to a rack to cool.

*Preparation time: 20 minutes*
*Yield: 12 to 14 servings*

# Mexican Chocolate Cake

This very dark, easily prepared spice cake gets its name from Mexican chocolate, which is flavored with cinnamon. Coffee liqueur also lends an exotic taste to this cake. Try the cake with a scoop of coffee ice cream, sprinkled with a mixture of shaved chocolate and a touch of cinnamon.

- 1 **stick (¹/₂ cup) butter or margarine, softened**
- 1 **cup brown sugar, preferably dark**
- 2 **eggs**
- 1 **teaspoon vanilla**
- ¹/₃ **cup coffee liqueur**
- ¹/₃ **cup water**
- 1¹/₂ **cups flour**
- 2 **teaspoons baking powder**
- 1 **teaspoon cinnamon**
- ¹/₈ **salt**
- 1 **cup finely ground semisweet chocolate**

1. Preheat the oven to 350°F.
2. Grease and flour an 8" square baking pan.
3. In a large bowl, cream the butter or margarine with the brown sugar until the sugar is fully incorporated. Beat in the eggs, then the vanilla, coffee liqueur, and water.
4. In another bowl, stir together the flour, baking powder, cinnamon, and salt. Add to the

creamed mixture, stirring until the dry ingredients are incorporated. Stir in the ground chocolate.

5. Spread the batter evenly in the prepared pan. Bake the cake for 40 minutes or until a toothpick inserted in the center comes out clean. Transfer the pan to a rack to cool.

*Preparation time: 20 minutes*
*Yield: 8 to 10 servings*

# CHAPTER FIVE

# NUT CAKES

The addition of nuts enhances many types of recipes. Consider, for example, Trout Almondine, Waldorf Salad, Pecan-Crusted Chicken, and Banana-Nut Bread. So it's not surprising that many cakes throughout this book are made crunchier and more tasty by the addition of nuts. The recipes in this chapter, however, use nuts to provide the predominant flavor and texture.

While the taste of different nuts is remarkably dissimilar, most nuts, when ground or chopped, are quite alike in their texture. As an experiment, I took one of my favorite recipes from this chapter, the Marbled Nut Cake, which calls for walnuts, and made it with pecans and then with almonds. Each time, it tasted different, but all versions were delicious.

So, if you prefer one nut to another in a recipe, by all means make that substitution. (In recipes calling for both almonds and almond extract, you may wish to eliminate the extract if you substitute a different nut.)

# Pecan-Crusted Pound Cake

This is a lovely pound cake that's made special by sprinkling the baking pan with pecans and chocolate. Although the cake may be baked in an ordinary tube pan, it is particularly attractive if you use a fluted Bundt pan. Note that no sugar is added to the unsweetened chocolate that lines the pan. Be assured, though, that the cake itself is sufficiently sweet to compensate for this.

| | |
|---|---|
| 1½ | cups finely chopped pecans |
| 1 | 1-ounce square unsweetened chocolate, finely grated or ground |
| 2 | sticks (1 cup) butter or margarine, softened (try to use at least half butter) |
| 1½ | cups sugar |
| 4 | eggs |
| ¾ | cup milk |
| 1 | teaspoon vanilla |
| 2 | cups flour |
| 1 | tablespoon baking powder |
| ¼ | teaspoon salt |

1. Grease and flour a tube or Bundt pan. Sprinkle the pecans and chocolate into the pan, and rotate the pan so they cover the bottom and sides.
2. Preheat the oven to 350°F.
3. In a large bowl, cream the butter or margarine

174

with the sugar until the sugar is fully incorporated. Beat in the eggs, then the milk and vanilla.

4. In another bowl, stir together the flour, baking powder, and salt. Add to the creamed mixture, stirring until the dry ingredients are incorporated.
5. Carefully spoon the batter into the prepared pan. Bake the cake for 1 hour 10 minutes or until a toothpick inserted in the highest part of the cake comes out clean. Transfer the pan to a rack to cool.

*Preparation time: 25 minutes*
*Yield: 12 to 14 servings*

# Marbled Nut Cake

Most marble cakes mix chocolate and vanilla batters. But this version is more subtle — the marbled batter contains ground walnuts with just a hint of chocolate and dark rum. It's a sophisticated dessert that would be even more delicious covered with Creamy White Icing (page 334); scatter additional chopped walnuts over the icing.

## MARBLING MIXTURE
- 1½ cups finely ground walnuts
- ¼ cup unsweetened cocoa powder
- ¼ cup milk
- 1 tablespoon dark rum

## CAKE
- 2 sticks (1 cup) butter or margarine, softened (try to use at least half butter)
- 1⅓ cups sugar
- 4 eggs
- 1½ teaspoons vanilla
- 2¼ cups flour
- 2 teaspoons baking powder
- 2 tablespoons dark rum (for sprinkling over baked cake)

1. To make the marbling mixture, in a large bowl, mix together all the marbling-mixture ingredients. Set aside.

2. Preheat the oven to 350°F.
3. Grease and flour a tube pan.
4. To make the cake, in another large bowl, cream the butter or margarine with the sugar until the sugar is fully incorporated. Beat in the eggs, then the vanilla.
5. In another bowl, stir together the flour and baking powder. Add to the creamed mixture, stirring until the dry ingredients are incorporated.
6. Transfer about half the batter into the bowl with the marbling mixture, and mix well.
7. Drop about 4 large spoonfuls of plain batter into the prepared pan, and cover with an equal amount of the nut batter. Continue adding batters to the pan in the same manner until the batters are used up. With a knife, swirl the batters gently to create a marbled effect.
8. Bake the cake for 1 hour 10 minutes or until a toothpick inserted in the highest part of the cake comes out clean. Sprinkle the cake with the 2 tablespoons rum. Transfer the pan to a rack to cool.

*Preparation time: 25 minutes*
*Yield: 12 to 14 servings*

# Sugared Walnut Cake

The sugar sprinkled over the top before baking gives this ultrarich walnut cake an attractive finish that's almost like a glaze. This is a quickly prepared cake that needs no additional icing.

|       |                                                       |
|-------|-------------------------------------------------------|
| 1     | stick (½ cup) butter or margarine, softened           |
| 1½    | cups plus 3 tablespoons sugar, divided usage          |
| 2     | eggs                                                  |
| 1     | cup heavy cream or whipping cream                      |
| 2     | teaspoons vanilla                                     |
| 2     | cups flour                                            |
| 2     | teaspoons baking powder                               |
| ¼     | teaspoon salt                                         |
| 1     | cup finely ground walnuts                             |

1. Preheat the oven to 350°F.
2. Grease and flour a tube pan.
3. In a large bowl, cream the butter or margarine with the 1½ cups of sugar until the sugar is fully incorporated. Beat in the eggs, then the cream and vanilla.
4. In another bowl, stir together the flour, baking powder, and salt. Add to the creamed mixture, stirring until the dry ingredients are incorporated. Stir in the walnuts.
5. Turn the batter out into the prepared pan. Sprinkle the top with the remaining 3 table-

spoons of sugar. Bake the cake for 1 hour or until a toothpick inserted in the highest part of the cake comes out clean. Transfer the pan to a rack to cool.

*Preparation time: 20 minutes*
*Yield: 12 to 14 servings*

# Walnut Butter Cake

Easy to make, this cake has a delicious buttery flavor enhanced by plenty of walnuts. The cake is great plain or with a scoop of ice cream.

> 2 **sticks (1 cup) butter or margarine, softened (try to use at least half butter)**
> 2 **cups sugar**
> 5 **eggs**
> 1 **tablespoon vanilla**
> 2 **cups flour**
> 1 **tablespoon baking powder**
> 1½ **cups finely chopped walnuts**

1. Preheat the oven to 350°F.
2. Grease and flour a 9" x 13" baking pan.
3. In a large bowl, cream the butter or margarine with the sugar until the sugar is fully incorporated. Beat in the eggs, then the vanilla.
4. In another bowl, stir together the flour and baking powder. Add to the creamed mixture, stirring until the dry ingredients are incorporated. Stir in the walnuts.
5. Spread the batter evenly in the prepared pan. Bake the cake for 1 hour or until a toothpick inserted in the center comes out clean. Transfer the pan to a rack to cool.

*Preparation time: 15 minutes*
*Yield: 12 to 15 servings*

# Greek Honey Cake

This cake has the flavor of baklava without all the work or the sticky sweetness. Just enough honey syrup is poured over a walnut butter cake to make it wonderfully moist. The cake stays fresh for days.

*Note:* If you are unable to locate orange flower water, you can omit it. The taste will be slightly less exotic.

## CAKE

|       |                                             |
|-------|---------------------------------------------|
| 2     | sticks (1 cup) butter or margarine, softened |
| 1½    | cups sugar                                  |
| 5     | eggs                                        |
| 2½    | cups flour                                  |
| 2     | teaspoons baking powder                     |
| 1½    | teaspoons cinnamon                          |
| 2½    | cups chopped walnuts                        |

## HONEY SYRUP

|     |                                                                                          |
|-----|------------------------------------------------------------------------------------------|
| ½   | cup sugar                                                                                |
| 1   | cup water                                                                                |
| ¼   | cup honey                                                                                |
| 1   | teaspoon orange flower water (available in pharmacies and Middle Eastern grocery stores) |

1. Preheat the oven to 350°F.
2. Grease and flour a 9" X 13" baking pan.

3. To make the cake, in a large bowl, cream the butter or margarine with the sugar until the sugar is fully incorporated. Beat in the eggs.
4. In another bowl, stir together the flour, baking powder, and cinnamon. Add to the creamed mixture, stirring until the dry ingredients are incorporated. Stir in the walnuts.
5. Spread the batter evenly in the prepared pan. Bake the cake for 45 minutes or until a tooth-pick inserted in the center comes out clean.
6. While the cake is baking, make the honey syrup. In a small saucepan, combine all the syrup ingredients. Bring to a boil. Lower the heat, and simmer, uncovered, about 7 minutes. Pour the syrup over the cake as soon as the cake comes out of the oven.

*Preparation time: 25 minutes*
*Yield: 16 servings*

# Linzer Cake

Linzertorte is a pie-like pastry with a spicy nut crust, raspberry-jam filling, and lattice topping. I decided to take these same delicious ingredients and transform them into a cake. And the result is great as well as far easier to prepare than its pastry counterpart. This walnut cake is spread with a thin layer of raspberry jam and is topped with a buttery streusel. The chocolate in the cake and topping complements the raspberry jam beautifully.

1½ **sticks (³/₄ cup) butter or margarine, softened**
1½ **cups sugar**
2 **cups flour**
2 **teaspoons baking powder**
1 **teaspoon cinnamon**
⅛ **teaspoon salt**
1½ **cups finely ground walnuts**
3 **ounces semisweet chocolate, ground (about ½ cup)**
2 **eggs**
⅔ **cup milk**
½ **cup seedless raspberry jam**

1. Preheat the oven to 350°F.
2. Grease and flour an 8" x 10" baking pan.
3. In a large bowl, cream the butter or margarine with the sugar until the sugar is fully in-

corporated.

4. In another bowl, stir together the flour, baking powder, cinnamon, salt, walnuts, and chocolate. Add to the creamed mixture, stirring until the dry ingredients are incorporated. The mixture will be crumbly. Remove 2 cups of this mixture, and set aside.

5. To the mixture remaining in the bowl, add the eggs and milk. Beat until fully incorporated.

6. Pour this batter into the prepared pan. Dot the batter with tiny spoonfuls of the raspberry jam. Using a knife, spread the jam into a thin layer. Sprinkle the reserved crumb mixture evenly over the jam.

7. Bake the cake for 1 hour 10 minutes or until a toothpick inserted in the center comes out clean. Transfer the pan to a rack to cool.

*Preparation time: 25 minutes*
*Yield: 15 servings*

# Crunchy Almond Cake

Whipped cream substitutes for butter in this freshly flavored, light cake. Half the almonds are sprinkled on the bottom of the pan, while the rest are folded into the batter. Not too sweet, this cake goes well with an afternoon cup of tea.

   $3/4$  **cup chopped almonds, divided usage**
   1  **cup heavy cream or whipping cream**
   1  **cup sugar**
   2  **eggs**
   1  **teaspoon vanilla**
   $1/4$  **teaspoon almond extract**
$1^1/_2$  **cups flour**
   2  **teaspoons baking powder**
   $1/8$  **teaspoon salt**

1. Preheat the oven to 350°F.
2. Generously butter a 9" x 5" loaf pan. Sprinkle half the almonds on the bottom. Reserve the remaining almonds.
3. In a large bowl, whip the cream until thick. Beat in the sugar until incorporated. Then beat in the eggs, vanilla, and almond extract.
4. In another bowl, stir together the flour, baking powder, and salt. Add to the cream mixture, stirring until the dry ingredients are incorporated. Stir in the remaining almonds.
5. Spread the batter evenly in the prepared pan. Bake the cake for 1 hour 5 minutes or until a

toothpick inserted in the center comes out clean. Transfer the pan to a rack to cool.

*Preparation time: 20 minutes*
*Yield: 8 servings*

# Almond Biscotti Cake

This takes the flavor of classic almond biscotti and puts it into a lovely golden cake. The combination of ground almonds and almond paste makes for an intensely almond-flavored cake, which goes well with a platter of fresh fruits. This is a quick and easy cake to prepare.

    9  **tablespoons butter or margarine, softened**
   ¾  **cup sugar**
    6  **eggs**
 1½  **teaspoons vanilla**
    1  **8-ounce can almond paste, cut into large cubes**
    1  **cup flour**
 1½  **teaspoons baking powder**
    1  **cup ground almonds**

1. Preheat the oven to 325°F.
2. Grease and flour a tube pan.
3. In a large bowl, cream the butter or margarine with the sugar until the sugar is fully incorporated. Beat in the eggs, then the vanilla. Add the almond paste, and continue beating until the mixture is smooth.
4. In another bowl, stir together the flour and baking powder. Add to the almond mixture, stirring until the dry ingredients are incorporated. Stir in the ground almonds.

5. Turn the batter into the prepared pan. Bake the cake for 1 hour 15 minutes or until a toothpick inserted in the highest part of the cake comes out clean. Transfer the pan to a rack to cool.

*Preparation time: 20 minutes*
*Yield: 8 to 10 servings*

# Toasted Nut Cake

Almonds and coconut, toasted until browned, combine in this deliciously crunchy cake. Since, unlike most cakes baked in a tube pan, this one is not large, it's perfect for those who find it too tempting to have cake around the house for several days. Chocolate–Sour Cream Icing (page 335) or Dark Chocolate Glaze (page 341) would be excellent frostings for this cake.

  1  **cup sweetened shredded coconut**
  1  **cup chopped almonds**
  2  **eggs**
 ¾  **cup sugar**
  1  **stick (½ cup) butter or margarine, melted**
  1  **cup plain low-fat yogurt**
 ½  **teaspoon almond extract**
1½  **cups flour**
  1  **teaspoon baking soda**
 ¼  **teaspoon salt**

1. Preheat the oven to 350°F.
2. Grease and flour a tube pan.
3. Spread the coconut and almonds on a large baking sheet, and bake 12 to 15 minutes, stirring occasionally Watch closely since the coconut and almonds can go from toasted to burnt very, very quickly. Remove from the pan as soon as they have browned or they will

continue to toast from the pan's heat.

4. In a large bowl, beat the eggs. Gradually beat in the sugar until the mixture is thick and pale yellow. Beat in the butter or margarine, then the yogurt and almond extract.

5. In another bowl, stir together the flour, baking soda, and salt. Add to the egg mixture, stirring until the dry ingredients are incorporated. Stir in the coconut and almonds.

6. Turn the batter out into the prepared pan. Bake the cake for 35 minutes or until a toothpick inserted in the highest part of the cake comes out clean. Transfer the pan to a rack to cool.

*Preparation time: 25 minutes*
*Yield: 10 servings*

# Chocolate-Coated Coconut Cake

Look at the ingredients in this recipe, and you'll know why this is one of the richest cakes in the book. For anyone who loves coconut, this cake is pure heaven. The chocolate coating not only makes for a very attractive cake, but gives it the flavor of a Mounds candy bar.

## CAKE

- 2 sticks (1 cup) butter or margarine, softened
- 2 cups sugar
- 5 eggs
- 1 cup sour cream
- 1 teaspoon vanilla
- 1 teaspoon coconut extract
- 2½ cups flour
- 2 teaspoons baking powder
- 1 teaspoon baking soda
- ⅛ teaspoon salt
- 1 cup shredded coconut

## TOPPING

- 4 ounces semisweet chocolate, melted
- ⅓ cup shredded coconut

1. Preheat the oven to 350°F.
2. Grease and flour a tube pan.
3. To make the cake, in a large bowl, cream the butter or margarine with the sugar until the

sugar is fully incorporated. Beat in the eggs, then the sour cream, vanilla, and coconut extract.

4. In another bowl, stir together the flour, baking powder, baking soda, and salt. Add to the creamed mixture, stirring until the dry ingredients are incorporated. Stir in the 1 cup of coconut.

5. Turn the batter out into the prepared pan. Bake the cake for 1 hour or until a toothpick inserted in the highest part of the cake comes out clean. Transfer the pan to a rack to cool.

6. When the cake has cooled completely, remove it from the pan. Pour the melted chocolate over the cake, and let it drip down the sides. Sprinkle the cake with the $1/3$ cup of coconut.

*Preparation time: 25 minutes*
*Yield: 16 servings*

# Butter Pecan Coffee Cake

Pecans are enveloped in a caramelized, baked-on topping that adorns a not-too-sweet cake studded with yet more pecans. This coffee cake, served warm from the oven or at room temperature, satisfies anyone's need for something special at breakfast.

## CAKE
- 6 eggs
- 1 cup sugar
- 1 cup brown sugar, preferably dark
- 1 stick ($\frac{1}{2}$ cup) butter or margarine, melted
- $\frac{1}{3}$ cup milk
- 2 teaspoons vanilla
- 3 cups flour
- 1 tablespoon baking powder
- $\frac{3}{4}$ cup chopped pecans

## TOPPING
- $5\frac{1}{3}$ tablespoons butter or margarine
- $\frac{1}{2}$ cup sugar
- $\frac{1}{2}$ cup light cream or half-and-half
- $\frac{3}{4}$ cup chopped pecans

1. Preheat the oven to 350°F.
2. Grease and flour a 9" x 13" baking pan.
3. To make the cake, in a large bowl, beat the eggs. Gradually beat in the sugar and brown

sugar until the mixture is thick. Beat in the butter or margarine, then the milk and vanilla.

4. In another bowl, stir together the flour and baking powder. Add to the egg mixture, stirring until the dry ingredients are incorporated. Stir in the pecans.
5. Spread the batter evenly in the prepared pan. Bake the cake for 40 minutes. The cake will be set and lightly browned on top, but it will not be completely baked.
6. While the cake is baking, make the topping. In a medium-sized skillet, combine the butter or margarine, sugar, and light cream or half-and-half. Bring to a boil, stirring. Then boil, uncovered, for 3 minutes.
7. When the cake comes out of the oven, pour the topping over it, and sprinkle with the pecans. Return the cake to the oven, and continue baking until the topping is light and bubbly, about 20 minutes. Transfer the pan to a rack to cool.

*Preparation time: 25 minutes*
*Yield: 20 to 24 servings*

# CHAPTER SIX

# REDUCED-FAT CAKES

Let's get our priorities straight: cake was never intended to be a health food. Rather, it's an indulgence — a sweet that should be enjoyed in moderation.

Wouldn't we be happier, though, if cakes were healthier? Sadly, when luscious, buttery fat is removed from baked goods, the results are usually dry and tasteless. While a few commercial manufacturers have succeeded in preserving a rich taste after removing the fat from cakes and cookies, home cooks don't yet have the means to accomplish this feat.

What we do have, though, is the opportunity to *lower* the fat content of cakes by substituting fruit purees for up to half the butter called for in a recipe. Depending on the particular cake, the results can be more than satisfactory — they can be downright delicious!

Here are some general tips for reducing the fat content of cakes:

- You can substitute pureed prunes for up to half the amount of butter or margarine. (Other fruits may also be used, but I find the texture is less "buttery" than with prunes.) Thus, if a recipe calls for 2 sticks (1 cup) of butter, you can make the cake with 1 stick (½ cup) of

196

butter and ½ cup of pureed prunes.

- To prepare ½ cup of pureed prunes, gently place dried, pitted prunes up to the ½-cup mark of a 1-cup measuring cup. Fill in the air pockets between the prunes by adding water up to the ½-cup mark. Now, either let the prunes soak for several hours or overnight, or simmer them, covered, for 10 minutes. Then puree the prunes, along with the soaking liquid, in a food processor. Add them to the recipe when the remaining butter is called for.
- Hearty cakes benefit most from such substitutions. Thus, using prunes in a traditional fluffy white layer cake would not work as well as using them in a full-flavored spice cake. Dark chocolate cakes are also enhanced by the flavor, deep color, and moist texture of pureed prunes.

Some of the recipes in this chapter are quite low in total fat, while others rely on fruit purees only to convert what otherwise would be a high-fat cake to one with a more reasonable fat content. Also, the fruit flavor is very noticeable in some cakes; in others — particularly those with chocolate — the puree adds only the barest hint of fruitiness. (My daughter, who has an intense dislike of prunes, is more than willing to partake of any chocolate cake in this chapter.)

One final comment: despite the amount of fat that has been eliminated from these cakes, all are delicious, and no one could ever accuse them of being "compromise" desserts.

# Almost-Fat-Free Chocolate Cake

This cake is so dark and chocolaty that the pureed prunes are almost undetectable. The cake is great right out of the oven. It will also keep well for several days. To enhance the chocolate flavor, frost with Dark Chocolate Glaze (page 341).

*Note:* To lower the fat content of this cake even more, substitute 4 egg whites for the 2 whole eggs.

| | |
|---|---|
| ½ | **stick (4 tablespoons) butter or margarine, softened** |
| ⅓ | **cup pureed prunes (see page 197)** |
| 2 | **cups sugar** |
| 2 | **eggs** |
| 1 | **cup nonfat milk** |
| 1 | **cup boiling water** |
| 1¾ | **cups flour** |
| ¾ | **cup unsweetened cocoa powder, sifted if lumpy** |
| ½ | **teaspoon baking soda** |
| 1½ | **teaspoons baking powder** |
| ⅛ | **teaspoon salt** |

1. Preheat the oven to 350°F.
2. Grease and flour a 9" x 13" baking pan.
3. In a large bowl, cream the butter or margarine and pureed prunes with the sugar until the sugar is fully incorporated. Beat in the eggs, then the milk and boiling water.

198

4. In another bowl, stir together the flour, cocoa, baking soda, baking powder, and salt. Beat into the creamed mixture, stirring until the dry ingredients are incorporated.
5. Spread the batter evenly in the prepared pan. Bake the cake for 35 minutes or until a toothpick inserted in the center comes out clean. Transfer the pan to a rack to cool.

*Preparation time: 25 minutes*
*Yield: 14 to 16 servings*

# Chocolate Snackin' Cake

In this cake, a homemade applesauce mixture is substituted for some of the usual butter or margarine. The result is a chocolate cake that's just as satisfying as its high-fat counterparts. This cake is delicious either warm from the oven or cold from the refrigerator, when you're hit with middle-of-the-night cravings. Cover the cake with Dark Chocolate Glaze (page 341), if you wish.

    1  **cup peeled, cored, and chopped apples**
 1¹/₃  **cups water**
    1  **cup rolled oats**
    1  **stick (¹/₂ cup) butter or margarine, softened**
    1  **cup sugar**
    1  **cup brown sugar, preferably dark**
    2  **eggs**
 1¹/₄  **cups flour**
 1¹/₄  **cups whole-wheat flour**
  ¹/₂  **cup unsweetened cocoa powder, sifted if lumpy**
    1  **teaspoon baking powder**
  ¹/₂  **teaspoon baking soda**
  ¹/₄  **teaspoon cinnamon**
  ¹/₂  **cup chopped walnuts**

1. Place the apples and water in a saucepan. Bring to a boil. Stir in the oats, and cover the pot.

Remove the pot from the heat, and let sit for 15 minutes.
2. Preheat the oven to 350°F.
3. Grease and flour a 9" X 13" baking pan.
4. In a large bowl, cream the butter or margarine with the sugar and brown sugar until the sugars are fully incorporated. Beat in the eggs, then the apple mixture.
5. In another bowl, stir together the flour, whole-wheat flour, cocoa, baking powder, baking soda, and cinnamon. Add to the apple mixture, stirring until the dry ingredients are incorporated. Stir in the walnuts.
6. Spread the batter evenly in the prepared pan. Bake the cake for 45 minutes or until a toothpick inserted in the center comes out clean. Transfer the pan to a rack to cool.

*Preparation time: 30 minutes*
*Yield: 16 servings*

# Fudgy Chocolate Cake

Here's another version of a low-fat chocolate cake, one which relies on applesauce as a substitute for butter. The applesauce lends a pleasant, fruity flavor to this quickly made cake.

 2 eggs
 1½ cups sugar
 ¼ cup vegetable oil
 1½ cups canned applesauce
 1 tablespoon vanilla
 ¾ cup evaporated skim milk
 1¾ cups flour
 ½ cup unsweetened cocoa powder, sifted if lumpy
 2 teaspoons baking powder
 ¼ teaspoon baking soda

1. Preheat the oven to 350°F.
2. Grease and flour a 9" square baking pan.
3. In a large bowl, beat the eggs. Gradually beat in the sugar until the mixture is thick and pale yellow. Beat in the oil, then the applesauce, vanilla, and evaporated milk.
4. In another bowl, stir together the flour, cocoa, baking powder, and baking soda. Add to the applesauce mixture, stirring until the dry ingredients are incorporated.
5. Turn the batter out into the prepared pan. Bake the cake for 1¼ hours or until a toothpick

inserted in the center comes out clean. Transfer the pan to a rack to cool.

*Preparation time: 20 minutes*
*Yield: 12 to 14 servings*

# Guiltless Brownies

These brownies contain only 1 egg yolk (instead of the usual 2), 3 tablespoons of oil (compared to about ⅓ cup of butter for most recipes), and fat-free cream cheese. But because they're made with real chocolate, the brownies are rich-tasting and thoroughly satisfying. They are also very chocolaty since the cream cheese adds body and texture rather than a cheese flavor.

## CREAM CHEESE MIXTURE

- 3 ounces fat-free cream cheese, softened
- ¼ cup sugar
- 1 tablespoon flour
- ½ teaspoon vanilla

## BROWNIES

- 1 egg
- 2 egg whites
- ¾ cup sugar
- 3 tablespoons vegetable oil
- 2 1-ounce squares unsweetened chocolate, melted
- 1 teaspoon vanilla
- ½ cup flour
- ½ teaspoon baking powder
- ⅛ teaspoon salt

1. To make the cream cheese mixture, in a small bowl, stir together all the cream-cheese-mixture ingredients. Set aside.
2. Preheat the oven to 350°F.
3. Grease and flour an 8" square baking pan.
4. To make the brownies, in a large bowl, beat the egg and egg whites. Gradually beat in the sugar until the mixture is thick. Beat in the oil, then the melted chocolate and vanilla.
5. In a small bowl, stir together the flour, baking powder, and salt. Add to the chocolate mixture, stirring until the dry ingredients are incorporated.
6. Spread the brownie batter evenly in the prepared pan. Top with spoonfuls of the cream cheese mixture. With a knife, swirl the cream cheese mixture into the brownie batter until no large lumps of cheese mixture can be seen.
7. Bake the brownies for 30 to 35 minutes or until a toothpick inserted in the center comes out almost clean. Transfer the pan to a rack to cool. When cool, cut into squares.

*Preparation time: 30 minutes*
*Yield: 12 to 16 brownies*

# Chocolate Carrot Cake

Restaurant-style carrot cake is one of the most fat-laden desserts you can eat, often containing more than a cup of oil. Pureed prunes reduce the fat content of this carrot cake, while cocoa lends a warm chocolate richness. Best with Vanilla Frosting (page 340), which has far less fat than the customary cream cheese frosting.

- 4 eggs
- 2 cups sugar
- 1 stick ($\frac{1}{2}$ cup) butter or margarine, melted
- $\frac{2}{3}$ cup pureed prunes (see page 197)
- $\frac{1}{2}$ cup orange juice
- 1 tablespoon grated orange peel
- 2 large carrots, peeled and shredded (about $1\frac{1}{2}$ cups)
- 1 cup flour
- 1 cup whole-wheat flour
- $\frac{2}{3}$ cup unsweetened cocoa powder, sifted if lumpy
- 1 teaspoon baking soda
- $1\frac{1}{2}$ teaspoons cinnamon
- $\frac{1}{2}$ teaspoon nutmeg
- 1 cup raisins
- 1 cup chopped walnuts

1. Preheat the oven to 350°F.
2. Grease and flour a tube pan.

3. In a large bowl, beat the eggs. Gradually beat in the sugar until the mixture is thick and pale yellow. Beat in the melted butter or margarine and pureed prunes, then the orange juice, orange peel, and carrots.
4. In another bowl, stir together the flour, whole-wheat flour, cocoa, baking soda, cinnamon, and nutmeg. Add to the carrot mixture, stirring until the dry ingredients are incorporated. Stir in the raisins and walnuts.
5. Turn the batter out into the prepared pan. Bake the cake for 1½ hours or until a toothpick inserted in the highest part of the cake comes out clean. Transfer the pan to a rack to cool.

*Preparation time: 30 minutes*
*Yield: 14 to 16 servings*

# Mocha Cake

For those who aren't crazy about prunes, the intense flavor of coffee liqueur almost completely masks their taste. All that remains is the buttery texture, making the cake dark and richly satisfying, even though it's very low in fat. To make it even more chocolaty, ice the cake with Dark Chocolate Glaze (page 341).

- ³/₄ **cup pureed prunes**
- 1 **cup coffee liqueur**
- 2 **eggs**
- 1 **cup sugar**
- ¹/₃ **cup vegetable oil**
- 1 **cup buttermilk or 1 tablespoon vinegar in a measuring cup plus milk up to the 1-cup mark**
- 1 **teaspoon vanilla**
- 1¹/₄ **cups flour**
- ¹/₃ **cup unsweetened cocoa powder, sifted if lumpy**
- 1 **teaspoon baking soda**

1. Place the prunes and coffee liqueur in a small saucepan. Bring to a full boil. Remove from the heat, and let cool slightly.
2. Preheat the oven to 350°F.
3. Grease and flour a tube pan.
4. Place the prunes and liqueur in the container of a food processor or blender, and process

until the prunes are very finely pureed. Add the eggs and sugar, and process until smooth. Add the oil, and process again. Add the buttermilk and vanilla, and process until incorporated.

5. In a large bowl, stir together the flour, cocoa, and baking soda. Add the contents of the food processor or blender, and stir until the dry ingredients are incorporated.

6. Turn the batter out into the prepared pan. Bake the cake for 1 hour or until a toothpick inserted in the highest part of the cake comes out clean. Transfer the pan to a rack to cool.

*Preparation time: 15 minutes*
*Yield: 10 servings*

# New-Way Gingerbread

This spicy, dark gingerbread provides the perfect disguise for the pureed prunes, which replace an entire stick of butter. This gingerbread is so delicious, I doubt anyone will distinguish it from the traditional gingerbread. New-Way Gingerbread can be served warm from the oven, plain, or with a dollop of applesauce. For a real treat, let the cake cool completely, then cover it with Dark Chocolate Glaze (page 341).

- 1/3 **cup (5 1/3 tablespoons) butter or margarine, softened**
- 1/2 **cup pureed prunes (see page 197)**
- 3/4 **cup brown sugar, preferably dark**
- 3/4 **cup molasses**
- 2 **eggs**
- 1 1/2 **cups flour**
- 1 1/4 **cups whole-wheat flour**
- 1 **teaspoon cinnamon**
- 1 **teaspoon ginger**
- 1/4 **teaspoon ground cloves**
- 1 **teaspoon baking soda**
- 1 **cup hot black coffee**

1. Preheat the oven to 350°F.
2. Grease and flour a 9" x 13" baking pan.
3. In a large bowl, cream the butter or margarine and pureed prunes with the brown sugar and molasses until the sugar is fully incorporated.

Beat in the eggs.

4. In another bowl, stir together the flour, whole-wheat flour, cinnamon, ginger, cloves, and baking soda. Add to the creamed mixture along with the coffee, stirring until the dry ingredients are incorporated.

5. Spread the batter evenly in the prepared pan. Bake the cake for 40 minutes or until a toothpick inserted in the center comes out clean. Transfer the pan to a rack to cool.

*Preparation time: 25 minutes*
*Yield: 16 servings*

# Mixed-Fruit Spice Cake

Pureed figs, mashed bananas, and applesauce are all substitutes for butter in this hearty spice cake that tastes like Fig Newtons.

*Note:* This cake should be stored in the refrigerator.

| | |
|---|---|
| 1 | cup dried figs, stems removed and quartered |
| 6 | tablespoons water |
| 2 | eggs |
| 1 | cup brown sugar, preferably dark |
| ¼ | cup vegetable oil |
| 1 | cup canned applesauce |
| 2 | ripe bananas, mashed |
| 1 | cup flour |
| 1 | cup whole-wheat flour |
| ¾ | teaspoon baking soda |
| 1 | teaspoon cinnamon |
| 1 | teaspoon ginger |
| ¼ | teaspoon nutmeg |

1. In a food processor or blender, puree the figs with the water.
2. Preheat the oven to 375°F.
3. Grease and flour a tube pan.
4. In a large bowl, beat the eggs. Gradually beat in the brown sugar until the mixture is thick. Beat in the oil, then the pureed figs, applesauce, and bananas.

5. In another bowl, stir together the flour, whole-wheat flour, baking soda, cinnamon, ginger, and nutmeg. Add to the fruit mixture, stirring until the dry ingredients are incorporated.
6. Turn the batter out into the prepared pan. Bake the cake for 1¼ hours or until a toothpick inserted in the highest part of the cake comes out clean. Transfer the pan to a rack to cool.

*Preparation time: 25 minutes*
*Yield: 14 to 16 servings*

# Cherry–Cream Cheese Cake

Instead of butter or margarine, this cake calls for fat-free cream cheese, which produces a satisfyingly dense texture. As you can see from the remaining ingredients, just a single egg yolk constitutes the entire fat content of the cake. This is a very fast cake to put together.

- 5 **ounces fat-free cream cheese, softened**
- ²/₃ **cup sugar**
- 1 **egg**
- 2 **egg whites**
- 1 **teaspoon vanilla**
- 1 **cup flour**
- 1 **teaspoon baking powder**
- 3 **ounces (about ¹/₂ cup) dried sweet cherries, coarsely chopped**

1. Preheat the oven to 350°F.
2. Grease and flour an 8" square baking pan.
3. In a large bowl, cream the cream cheese with the sugar until the sugar is fully incorporated. Beat in the egg and egg whites, then the vanilla.
4. In another bowl, stir together the flour and baking powder. Add to the cream cheese mixture, stirring until the dry ingredients are incorporated. Stir in the cherries.
5. Spread the batter in the prepared pan. Bake

the cake for 45 to 50 minutes or until a tooth-pick inserted in the center comes out clean. Transfer the pan to a rack to cool.

*Preparation time: 15 minutes*
*Yield: 8 to 9 servings*

# Apple Butter–Zucchini Cake

This is a hearty cake that gets its satisfying quality from apple butter and just ¼ cup of oil, rather than from butter or margarine. While the grated zucchini does not affect the cake's flavor, it does enhance its texture. Caramel Icing (page 336) would be a nice addition to this cake.

|     |                             |
| --- | --------------------------- |
| 3   | eggs                        |
| 1½  | cups sugar                  |
| ¼   | cup vegetable oil           |
| ½   | cup apple butter            |
| 1¼  | cups flour                  |
| 1¼  | cups whole-wheat flour      |
| ½   | cup rolled oats             |
| 1   | tablespoon baking powder    |
| 1½  | teaspoons cinnamon          |
| ¼   | teaspoon salt               |
| 2   | cups coarsely grated zucchini |
| ¼   | cup chopped walnuts         |

1. Preheat the oven to 350°F.
2. Grease and flour a tube pan.
3. In a large bowl, beat the eggs. Gradually beat in the sugar until the mixture is thick and pale yellow. Beat in the oil and apple butter.
4. In another bowl, stir together the flour, whole-wheat flour, oats, baking powder, cinnamon, and salt. Add to the apple butter mixture, stirring until the dry ingredients are incorporated.

Stir in the zucchini and walnuts.

5. Turn the batter out into the prepared pan. Bake the cake for 50 to 60 minutes or until a toothpick inserted in the highest part of the cake comes out clean. Transfer the pan to a rack to cool.

*Preparation time: 20 minutes*
*Yield: 16 servings*

# Aromatic Honey Cake

Considering that the fat contained in this cake amounts to just ¼ cup of oil and 2 egg yolks, the texture is lovely. And few people would guess that this is a low-fat dessert. Fragrant tea combined with honey and spices make for an unusually flavorful cake.

1 cup boiling water
1 "Constant Comment" tea bag or similar orange/spice-flavored tea
2 eggs
2 egg whites
1 cup sugar
1 cup honey
¼ cup vegetable oil
½ cup canned applesauce
1½ cups flour
1½ cups whole-wheat flour
2 teaspoons baking powder
1 teaspoon baking soda
1 teaspoon cinnamon
½ teaspoon ginger
⅛ teaspoon ground cloves

1. Pour the boiling water over the tea bag, and let steep until quite strong. Remove the tea bag.
2. Preheat the oven to 350°F.
3. Grease and flour a tube pan.

4. In a large bowl, beat the eggs and egg whites. Gradually beat in the sugar until the mixture is thick and pale. Beat in the honey, then the oil, applesauce, and tea.
5. In another bowl, stir together the flour, whole-wheat flour, baking powder, baking soda, cinnamon, ginger, and cloves. Add to the tea mixture, stirring until the dry ingredients are incorporated.
6. Turn the batter out into the prepared pan. Bake the cake for 1 hour 5 minutes or until a toothpick inserted in the highest part of the cake comes out clean. Transfer the pan to a rack to cool.

*Preparation time: 25 minutes*
*Yield: 16 servings*

# CHAPTER SEVEN

# BISCOTTI

Everyone loves cookies. Who doesn't count among his or her favorites Oreos, Fig Newtons, gingersnaps, and — most popular of all — chocolate chip? And most of us would also include biscotti.

Commercial versions of biscotti may be hard to locate. And when they are found — usually in specialty food stores — these crispy treats are generally more expensive than other store-bought cookies.

For the home baker, though, not only are biscotti as economical as any other homemade cookie, they are easier to make. While most cookies require an hour or more of careful vigilance as baking sheets go in and out of the oven, whipping up a batch of biscotti is more like baking a cake. (That's why they're included in this book.)

For anyone not familiar with how biscotti are made, the procedure is simple. Cookie-like dough is shaped into long, wide logs on a baking sheet. (The easiest way to do this is to drop onto the cookie sheet large spoonfuls of dough, which eventually assume the size and shape of logs. Then, with the side of a knife, the dough is molded into even log shapes.) The logs are baked until they are brown on the outside but not fully cooked through, and are then sliced and the slices laid on their sides. The biscotti go back into the oven to brown, first on one side and then on the other.

Generally, commercial biscotti are very crisp — often rather hard and dry. The biscotti recipes in this book, however, produce slices that are attractively toasted on each side but are still pleasantly chewy on the inside. (If you prefer drier biscotti, add an additional 15 to 20 minutes of baking time to any of these recipes, which will produce the desired texture.)

You'll notice that these biscotti recipes yield only 1 to 2 dozen slices, which might not seem like much if you're expecting the tiny, commercial variety of biscotti. But my biscotti are far more satisfying, a single one being sufficient for an ample serving.

Biscotti are great as a dessert with sorbet after dinner, with coffee or tea as a between-meal snack, as a delicious addition to your picnic basket, or whenever you want a sweet treat.

# Chocolate-Espresso Biscotti

Chocolate-covered espresso beans (available in candy shops) lend an intense mocha flavor and distinctive crunch to these dark chocolate biscotti. Needless to say, the biscotti are a marvelous accompaniment to after-dinner espresso and sorbet or gelati.

- 6 **tablespoons butter or margarine, softened**
- 1 **cup sugar**
- 2 **eggs**
- 2 **cups flour**
- ½ **cup unsweetened cocoa powder, sifted if lumpy**
- 1 **teaspoon baking powder**
- ¼ **teaspoon salt**
- 1 **cup chocolate-covered espresso beans**

1. Preheat the oven to 350°F.
2. Grease a large baking sheet.
3. In a large bowl, cream the butter or margarine with the sugar until the sugar is fully incorporated. Beat in the eggs.
4. In another bowl, stir together the flour, cocoa, baking powder, and salt. Add to the creamed mixture, stirring until the dry ingredients are incorporated. Stir in the espresso beans. (Since the dough will be very stiff, you may need to do this with your hands.)

5. On the prepared baking sheet, form the dough into two logs, each about 10" x 2". Bake the logs for 30 minutes.
6. Remove the baking sheet from the oven, and cut each log on the diagonal into 9 or 10 slices. Lay the slices on their side, and bake the biscotti for 10 minutes. Turn the slices over, and bake 5 minutes longer. Transfer the biscotti to a rack to cool.

*Preparation time: 25 minutes*
*Yield: 18 to 20 biscotti*

# Granola Biscotti

Crushed granola cereal adds a unique texture and flavor to these biscotti, which also contain maple syrup. Be certain to purchase cereal that contains fruits and nuts.

| | |
|---|---|
| 2 | **eggs** |
| 1/3 | **cup brown sugar, preferably dark** |
| 1/4 | **cup vegetable oil** |
| 1/4 | **cup maple syrup** |
| 1 | **teaspoon vanilla** |
| 1 1/2 | **cups granola cereal, crushed slightly in a food processor or with a rolling pin** |
| 1 1/2 | **cups flour** |
| 1 | **teaspoon baking powder** |
| 1/2 | **teaspoon baking soda** |
| 1/8 | **teaspoon salt** |

1. Preheat the oven to 325°F.
2. Grease a large baking sheet.
3. In a large bowl, beat the eggs. Gradually beat in the brown sugar until the mixture is thick and pale. Beat in the oil, then the maple syrup and vanilla.
4. In another bowl, stir together the granola, flour, baking powder, baking soda, and salt. Add to the egg mixture, stirring until the dry ingredients are incorporated.
5. On the prepared baking sheet, form the dough

into two logs, each about 8" X 3". Bake the logs for 20 minutes or until lightly browned.

6. Remove the baking sheet from the oven, and reduce the oven temperature to 300°F. Cut each log on the diagonal into 8 slices, each about 1" thick. Lay the slices on their side, and bake the biscotti for 15 minutes. Turn the slices over, and bake 15 minutes longer. Transfer the biscotti to a rack to cool.

*Preparation time: 25 minutes*
*Yield: 16 biscotti*

# Two-Nut Biscotti

These biscotti are amply filled with coconut and chopped walnuts. The result — partly because these biscotti have more butter than most — is a very rich version of this crunchy Italian cookie.

1 stick ($\frac{1}{2}$ cup) butter or margarine, softened
$\frac{3}{4}$ cup brown sugar, preferably dark
2 eggs
$2\frac{1}{4}$ cups flour
$1\frac{1}{2}$ teaspoons baking powder
$\frac{1}{8}$ teaspoon salt
$\frac{2}{3}$ cup shredded coconut
1 cup chopped walnuts

1. Preheat the oven to 350°F.
2. Grease a large baking sheet.
3. In a large bowl, cream the butter or margarine with the brown sugar until the sugar is fully incorporated. Beat in the eggs.
4. In another bowl, stir together the flour, baking powder, and salt. Add to the creamed mixture, stirring until the dry ingredients are incorporated. Stir in the coconut and walnuts.
5. On the prepared baking sheet, form the dough into two logs, each about 8" x 3". Bake the logs for 25 minutes or until lightly browned.
6. Remove the baking sheet from the oven, and reduce the oven temperature to 325°F. Cut

each log on the diagonal, into about 8 slices, each about 1" thick. Lay the slices on their side, and bake the biscotti for 10 minutes. Turn the slices over, and bake 5 minutes longer. Transfer the biscotti to a rack to cool.

*Preparation time: 25 minutes*
*Yield: 16 biscotti*

# Chip 'n' Nut Biscotti

Macadamia nuts and chocolate chips combine to make these the most luxurious of all biscotti. They are positively irresistible!

- 3 eggs
- ½ cup sugar
- ½ cup brown sugar, preferably dark
- ¼ cup vegetable oil
- 1 teaspoon vanilla
- 2 cups flour
- ½ teaspoon baking powder
- 1 cup mini-semisweet chocolate morsels or coarsely chopped regular-size morsels
- 1 4-ounce jar (¾ cup) lightly salted macadamia nuts, chopped

1. Preheat the oven to 350°F.
2. Grease a large baking sheet.
3. In a large bowl, beat the eggs. Gradually beat in the sugar and brown sugar until the mixture is thick and pale. Beat in the vegetable oil, then the vanilla.
4. In another bowl, stir together the flour and baking powder. Add to the egg mixture, stirring until the dry ingredients are incorporated. Stir in the chocolate and macadamias.
5. On the prepared baking sheet, form the dough into two logs, each about 12" x 3". Bake the

logs for 35 minutes or until lightly browned.
6. Remove the baking sheet from the oven, and reduce the oven temperature to 325°F. Cut each log on the diagonal into 10 to 12 slices. Lay the slices on their side, and bake the biscotti for 10 minutes. Turn the slices over, and bake 5 minutes longer. Transfer the biscotti to a rack to cool.

*Preparation time: 25 minutes*
*Yield: 20 to 24 biscotti*

# Toblerone Biscotti

Brown sugar and melted butter give these biscotti a butterscotch flavor, while the Toblerone candy bar adds honey, almonds, and dark chocolate. If you like chocolate chip cookies, you'll love these biscotti.

2 eggs
$^1/_2$ cup brown sugar, preferably dark
$^1/_3$ cup (5$^1/_3$ tablespoons) butter or margarine, melted
1 teaspoon vanilla
2$^1/_4$ cups flour
1 teaspoon baking powder
1 3.52-ounce bar bittersweet chocolate Toblerone, chopped

1. Preheat the oven to 350°F.
2. Grease a large baking sheet.
3. In a large bowl, beat the eggs. Gradually beat in the brown sugar until the mixture is thick and pale. Beat in the melted butter or margarine, then the vanilla.
4. In another bowl, stir together the flour and baking powder. Add to the egg mixture, stirring until the dry ingredients are incorporated. Stir in the chopped Toblerone bar.
5. On the prepared baking sheet, form the dough into two logs, each about 8" x 2$^1/_2$". Bake the logs for 25 minutes.

6. Remove the baking sheet from the oven, and reduce the oven temperature to 300°F. Cut each log on the diagonal into 7 or 8 slices. Lay the slices on their side, and bake the biscotti for 10 minutes. Turn the slices over, and bake 5 minutes longer. Transfer the biscotti to a rack to cool.

*Preparation time: 25 minutes*
*Yield: 14 to 16 biscotti*

# Lori's Butterscotch Biscotti

I've named these biscotti after my friend Lori not because she developed the recipe, but because she was so persistent in urging me to create a recipe to please the butterscotch lovers of this world. According to Lori, fans of butterscotch are legion and are mostly ignored. Unlike chocolate addicts, who can easily find a wealth of chocolate recipes to meet their cravings, people who long for the mellow flavor of butterscotch have to search hard for a good recipe. So for Lori and everyone else who loves butterscotch, this biscotti recipe is for you.

| | |
|---|---|
| 2 | eggs |
| 1 | cup brown sugar, preferably dark |
| 1 | stick (½ cup) butter or margarine, melted (try to use butter) |
| 2 | teaspoons vanilla |
| 2 | tablespoons water |
| 3 | cups flour |
| 2 | teaspoons baking powder |
| ¼ | teaspoon salt |
| ½ | cup chopped pecans |
| 1 | 6-ounce package butterscotch morsels |

1. Preheat the oven to 350°F.
2. Grease a large baking sheet.
3. In a large bowl, beat the eggs. Gradually beat

in the brown sugar until the mixture is thick and pale. Beat in the melted butter or margarine, then the vanilla and water.

4. In another bowl, stir together the flour, baking powder, and salt. Add to the egg mixture, stirring until the dry ingredients are incorporated. Stir in the pecans and butterscotch morsels.

5. On the prepared baking sheet, form the dough into two logs, each about 13" X 2½". Bake the logs for 30 minutes.

6. Remove the baking sheet from the oven, and reduce the oven temperature to 300°F. Cut each log on the diagonal into about 10 slices. Lay the slices on their side, and bake the biscotti for 15 minutes. Turn the slices over, and bake 10 minutes longer or until lightly browned. Transfer the biscotti to a rack to cool.

*Preparation time: 25 minutes*
*Yield: about 20 biscotti*

# Almond Biscotti

Almond is the traditional flavor for biscotti. These are larger and more satisfying than ones you'll find in restaurants or gourmet shops. While most biscotti contain whole almonds, this recipe uses ground nuts to lend a subtle flavor and texture to the cookie.

*Note:* Almonds can be easily ground in a food processor.

3 eggs
1 cup sugar
$1/4$ cup vegetable oil
2 teaspoons vanilla
$1/2$ teaspoon almond extract
2 cups flour
$1^1/2$ teaspoons baking powder
$1/2$ teaspoon baking soda
$1/8$ teaspoon salt
4 ounces almonds, ground (about $1/2$ cup slivered almonds before grinding)

1. Preheat the oven to 350°F.
2. Grease a large baking sheet.
3. In a large bowl, beat the eggs well. Gradually beat in the sugar until the mixture is thick and pale yellow. Beat in the oil, then the vanilla and almond extract.
4. In another bowl, stir together the flour, baking

powder, baking soda, salt, and almonds. Add to the egg mixture, stirring until the dry ingredients are incorporated.

5. On the prepared baking sheet, form the dough into two logs, each about 8" x 2½". Bake the logs for 20 to 25 minutes or until lightly browned and not sticky to the touch.

6. Remove the baking sheet from the oven, and reduce the oven temperature to 325°F. Cut each log on the diagonal into about 8 slices. Lay the slices on their side, and bake the biscotti for 10 minutes. Turn the slices over, and bake 5 minutes longer. Transfer the biscotti to a rack to cool.

*Preparation time: 25 minutes*
*Yield: about 16 biscotti*

# Amaretto Biscotti

These biscotti have a subtle almond flavor because of the addition of amaretto to the dough. They are also studded with whole almonds.

*Note:* If you prefer the taste of toasted almonds, spread the nuts on a baking sheet, and bake them in a 325°F oven until they are lightly browned. Remove them from the pan immediately. Or you may place the almonds in an ungreased skillet over a fairly high heat, and cook them, stirring them constantly, until they are browned. Remove the nuts from the pan immediately. Let them cool before adding them to the dough.

> 1 stick (½ cup) butter or margarine, softened
> ⅔ cup sugar
> 2 eggs
> 2 tablespoons amaretto liqueur
> 1 teaspoon vanilla
> 3 cups flour
> 2 teaspoons baking powder
> ¼ teaspoon salt
> 1 cup blanched whole almonds (see *Note,* above)

1. Preheat the oven to 325°F.
2. Grease a large baking sheet.
3. In a large bowl, cream the butter or margarine with the sugar until the sugar is fully incorpo-

rated. Beat in the eggs, then the amaretto and vanilla.

4. In another bowl, stir together the flour, baking powder, and salt. Add to the creamed mixture, stirring until the dry ingredients are incorporated. The dough will be quite stiff. Stir in the almonds.

5. On the prepared baking sheet, form the dough into two logs, each about 8" X 2½". Bake the logs for 30 minutes or until lightly browned.

6. Remove the baking sheet from the oven, and reduce the oven temperature to 300°F. Cut each log on the diagonal into 10 slices. Lay the slices on their side, and bake the biscotti for 15 minutes. Turn the slices over, and bake 15 minutes longer. Transfer the biscotti to a rack to cool.

*Preparation time: 25 minutes*
*Yield: 20 biscotti*

# Continental Biscotti

When I was growing up, the word Continental was synonymous with "sophisticated." With that in mind, I have named these Continental Biscotti, which contain the sophisticated combination of aniseeds, pine nuts, and chopped dried figs. Continental Biscotti make an elegant accompaniment to fresh berries, sorbet, or after-dinner cognac.

|   |   |
|---|---|
| 3 | eggs |
| 1 | cup sugar |
| 1 | stick (½ cup) butter or margarine, melted |
| 1 | tablespoon water |
| 1 | teaspoon vanilla |
| 2 | tablespoons brandy |
| 3 | cups flour |
| 1½ | teaspoons baking powder |
| 2 | teaspoons aniseeds |
| ½ | cup pine nuts |
| ½ | cup chopped dried figs |

1. Preheat the oven to 375°F.
2. Grease a baking sheet.
3. In a large bowl, beat the eggs. Gradually beat in the sugar until the mixture is thick and pale yellow. Beat in the melted butter or margarine, then the water, vanilla, and brandy.
4. In another bowl, stir together the flour, baking powder, and aniseeds. Add to the egg mixture,

stirring until the dry ingredients are incorporated. Stir in the pine nuts and dried figs.

5. On the prepared baking sheet, form the dough into two logs, each about 12" X 3". Bake the logs for 20 minutes.

6. Remove the baking sheet from the oven, and reduce the oven temperature to 300°F. Cut each log on the diagonal into about 12 slices. Lay the slices on their side, and bake the biscotti for 15 minutes. Turn the slices over, and bake 10 minutes longer. Transfer the biscotti to a rack to cool.

*Preparation time: 25 minutes*
*Yield: about 24 biscotti*

# Candied-Almond Biscotti

Classic almond biscotti are enhanced by adding whole almonds dipped in chocolate as well as Jordan almonds (with a hard sugar coating). Both the chocolate and sugar covering melt in the biscotti, adding a sweet burst of flavor.

*Note:* Both chocolate-covered almonds and Jordan almonds can be found in candy shops. Hershey also makes chocolate-covered Golden Almonds, available in most supermarkets.

|     |     |
| --- | --- |
| 2 | eggs |
| ¾ | cup sugar |
| ¼ | cup vegetable oil |
| ½ | teaspoon almond extract |
| 2 | cups flour |
| ½ | teaspoon baking powder |
| ½ | teaspoon baking soda |
| ½ | cup chocolate-covered almonds |
| ¼ | cup Jordan almonds |

1. Preheat the oven to 350°F.
2. Grease a large baking sheet.
3. In a large bowl, beat the eggs. Gradually beat in the sugar until the mixture is thick and pale yellow. Beat in the oil and almond extract.
4. In another bowl, stir together the flour, baking powder, and baking soda. Add to the egg mixture, stirring until the dry ingredients are incorporated. Stir in the chocolate-covered al-

monds and Jordan almonds.

5. On the prepared baking sheet, form the dough into two logs, each about 8" x 2". Bake the logs for 30 minutes or until the dough is no longer sticky.

6. Remove the baking sheet from the oven. Cut each log on the diagonal into 8 slices. Lay the slices on their side, and bake the biscotti for 5 minutes. Turn the slices over, and bake 5 minutes longer. Transfer the biscotti to a rack to cool.

*Preparation time: 25 minutes*
*Yield: 16 biscotti*

# Three Ps Biscotti

The "three Ps" are pepper, pecans, and pine nuts. Black pepper combined with chocolate lends a sophisticated "wake up" to the palate, pecans add crunch, and the pine nuts contribute a subtle flavor. These biscotti go well with a sorbet dessert or make an appealing mid-morning or tea-time treat.

|       |                                             |
|-------|---------------------------------------------|
| 3     | eggs                                        |
| 1¼    | cups sugar                                  |
| ¼     | cup vegetable oil                           |
| 2     | cups flour                                  |
| ½     | cup unsweetened cocoa powder, sifted if lumpy |
| ½     | teaspoon baking powder                      |
| ½     | teaspoon baking soda                        |
| ⅛     | teaspoon salt                               |
| 1     | teaspoon black pepper                       |
| ¾     | cup coarsely chopped pecans                 |
| ¼     | cup pine nuts                               |

1. Preheat the oven to 350°F.
2. Grease a large baking sheet.
3. In a large bowl, beat the eggs. Gradually beat in the sugar until the mixture is thick and pale yellow. Beat in the vegetable oil.
4. In another bowl, stir together the flour, cocoa, baking powder, baking soda, salt, and pepper. Add to the egg mixture, stirring until the dry

ingredients are incorporated. Stir in the pecans and pine nuts.
5. On the prepared baking sheet, form the dough into two logs, each about 8" X 3". Bake the logs for 30 minutes or until lightly browned and not sticky to the touch.
6. Remove the baking sheet from the oven, and reduce the oven temperature to 300°F. Cut each log on the diagonal into 9 slices. Lay the slices on their side, and bake the biscotti for 10 minutes. Turn the slices over, and bake 5 minutes longer. Transfer the biscotti to a rack to cool.

*Preparation time: 25 minutes*
*Yield: 18 biscotti*

# Lemon Biscotti

These poppy seed biscotti are attractive in many ways. In terms of flavor, the lemon peel adds a refreshing tang. In terms of having the ingredients around, even when your kitchen shelves are nearly bare, you're likely to have these ingredients on hand. And these cookies are a snap to make.

     2  **eggs**
    ¾  **cup sugar**
    ¼  **cup vegetable oil**
     1  **tablespoon grated lemon peel**
     2  **cups flour**
     3  **tablespoons poppy seeds**
    ½  **teaspoon baking powder**
    ½  **teaspoon baking soda**


1. Preheat the oven to 350°F.
2. Grease a large baking sheet.
3. In a large bowl, beat the eggs. Gradually beat in the sugar until the mixture is thick and pale yellow. Beat in the vegetable oil and lemon peel.
4. In another bowl, stir together the flour, poppy seeds, baking powder, and baking soda. Add to the lemon mixture, stirring until the dry ingredients are incorporated.
5. On the prepared baking sheet, form the dough into two logs, each about 8" x 2". Bake the logs for 30 minutes or until they are no longer

sticky to the touch.

6. Remove the baking sheet from the oven. Cut each log on the diagonal into 8 slices. Lay the slices on their side, and bake the biscotti for 5 minutes. Turn the slices over, and bake 5 minutes longer. Transfer the biscotti to a rack to cool.

*Preparation time: 20 minutes*
*Yield: 16 biscotti*

# White Chocolate–Cherry Biscotti

The white chocolate adds a richness not usually found in biscotti, while the dried cherries contribute a lovely fruity flavor. These are a delightful addition to any collection of biscotti recipes.

2 eggs
$^2/_3$ cup honey
$^1/_3$ cup vegetable oil
2 tablespoons water
1 teaspoon vanilla
$2^3/_4$ cups flour
1 teaspoon baking powder
$^1/_2$ teaspoon baking soda
$^1/_2$ cup (about 3 ounces) dried Bing cherries
2 1-ounce squares white baking chocolate, coarsely chopped

1. Preheat the oven to 325°F.
2. Grease a large baking sheet.
3. In a large bowl, beat the eggs. Gradually beat in the honey until the mixture is thick. Beat in the vegetable oil, then the water and vanilla.
4. In another bowl, stir together the flour, baking powder, and baking soda. Add to the honey mixture, stirring until the dry ingredients are incorporated. Stir in the cherries and white chocolate.
5. On the prepared baking sheet, form the dough

into two logs, each about 8" X 3". Bake the logs for 30 minutes or until lightly browned.

6. Remove the baking sheet from the oven, and reduce the oven temperature to 300°F. Cut each log on the diagonal into 10 slices. Lay the slices on their side, and bake the biscotti for 10 minutes. Turn the slices over, and bake 10 minutes longer. Transfer the biscotti to a rack to cool.

*Preparation time: 25 minutes*
*Yield: 20 biscotti*

# Two-Toned Biscotti

Here, the two most popular biscotti varieties — almond and chocolate — team up to create a very attractive and tasty treat.

*Note:* To toast the almonds, see page 236.

3 eggs
1 cup sugar
$1/4$ cup vegetable oil
1 teaspoon vanilla
2 cups flour
1 teaspoon baking powder
$1/2$ teaspoon baking soda
$1/8$ teaspoon salt
$1/2$ teaspoon almond extract
$1/2$ cup chopped almonds, toasted
1 1-ounce square unsweetened chocolate, melted
1 tablespoon unsweetened cocoa powder, sifted if lumpy
4 teaspoons water
2 teaspoons instant coffee powder

1. Preheat the oven to 325°F.
2. Grease a large baking sheet.
3. In a large bowl, beat the eggs. Gradually beat in the sugar until the mixture is thick and pale yellow. Beat in the vegetable oil, then the vanilla.
4. In another bowl, stir together the flour, baking

248

powder, baking soda, and salt. Add to the egg mixture, stirring until the dry ingredients are incorporated.

5. Divide the dough into two equal portions. To one portion, add the almond extract and toasted almonds. In a small bowl, stir together the melted chocolate, cocoa, water, and coffee powder. Add this to the other half of the dough.

6. Divide the almond dough and chocolate dough into two equal portions. Place half the almond dough on the prepared baking sheet, and shape it with your hands into a rectangle about 8" X 4". Place half the chocolate dough on top, and form it into an equal-size rectangle. Lightly press the two doughs together. Repeat this process with the remaining half of the almond dough and the remaining half of the chocolate dough. Bake the rectangles for 20 to 25 minutes or until they are no longer sticky to the touch.

7. Remove the baking sheet from the oven, and reduce the oven temperature to 300°F. Cut each log on the diagonal into 10 slices. Lay the slices on their side, and bake the biscotti for 15 minutes. Turn the slices over, and bake 15 minutes longer. Transfer the biscotti to a rack to cool.

*Preparation time: 30 minutes*
*Yield: 20 biscotti*

# CHAPTER EIGHT

# BAR CAKES

Although most cookbooks classify bars as cookies, to my way of thinking they are really extra-thin cakes. The batter is made the same way cake batters are. And bars require none of that tedious shaping, chilling, or dropping that are the hallmark of true cookies. There is also a fine line between a sheet cake and a cake that is cut into bars. So for these reasons and because I love bars and have amassed a great many recipes for them over the years, I am devoting this chapter to cakes of this type.

Bar cakes offer several advantages over other cakes:

- Because they are thin, they usually bake in a short amount of time and, therefore, are ready to be consumed sooner than a regular cake.
- Most bar cakes are also quite sturdy and so pack and mail well for gift giving.
- As an added bonus, because they are cut into individual portions, it's easy to make a single pan and give half as a gift, while saving some for yourself.
- Finally, bar cakes often have wonderful fillings or baked-on toppings that enhance their flavor, texture, and attractiveness.

# World's Best Brownies

Since I always see recipes for "the world's best" something, I figure that, as someone who has easily sampled scores of brownies made from dozens of recipes, I am just as qualified to add my contender for the title of World's Best Brownies. These brownies are dark and sensuously chewy. The batter contains cocoa as well as the usual unsweetened chocolate, the resulting brownie having the most intensely chocolaty flavor imaginable. After baking, the brownies are covered with a thin layer of caramel ice-cream topping and then sprinkled with pecans and shaved chocolate. It's like eating a brownie with a candy-bar topping.

*Note:* If you like to eat your brownies right from the oven, you can skip the caramel topping. Or, better yet, put a hot brownie square on a plate, pour a generous spoonful of caramel topping over it, and then sprinkle the brownie with pecans and grated chocolate.

|   |   |
|---|---|
| 2 | **1-ounce squares unsweetened chocolate** |
| 5$\frac{1}{3}$ | **tablespoons butter or margarine** |
| 2 | **eggs** |
| 1 | **cup sugar** |
| 1 | **teaspoon vanilla** |
| $\frac{2}{3}$ | **cup flour** |
| 3 | **tablespoons unsweetened cocoa powder, sifted if lumpy** |
| $\frac{1}{2}$ | **teaspoon baking powder** |
| $\frac{1}{8}$ | **teaspoon salt** |

$^1/_4$ **cup caramel ice-cream topping (such as Smucker's)**
$^1/_2$ **cup coarsely chopped pecans**
$^1/_2$ **cup shaved, grated, or finely chopped semisweet chocolate**

1. In a small, heavy saucepan, melt the chocolate and butter or margarine over low heat, stirring occasionally.
2. Preheat the oven to 350°F.
3. Grease and flour an 8" square baking pan.
4. In a large bowl, beat the eggs. Gradually beat in the sugar until the mixture is thick and pale yellow. Beat in the melted chocolate mixture, then the vanilla.
5. In another bowl, stir together the flour, cocoa, baking powder, and salt. Add to the chocolate mixture, stirring until the dry ingredients are incorporated.
6. Spread the batter evenly in the prepared pan. Bake the brownies for 25 minutes. The top will be shiny and cracked, and when you insert a toothpick into the center of the brownies, it will come out nearly, but not completely, clean. Transfer the brownies to a rack to cool.
7. When completely cool, spread the brownies with the caramel topping. Sprinkle with the pecans and chocolate, and press down lightly. Cut into squares.

*Preparation time: 20 minutes*
*Yield: 13 to 16 brownies*

# Double-Chocolate Shortbread Squares

Scottish shortbread is so rich and buttery, the only possible way to improve it is to add chocolate — here found in both the shortbread itself and in the candy-like topping.

    1  stick (¹/₂ cup) butter or margarine,
        softened (try to use at least half
        butter)
    1  cup sugar
    1  egg
    1  teaspoon vanilla
 1¹/₂  cups flour
    2  tablespoons cornstarch
    6  tablespoons unsweetened cocoa
        powder, sifted if lumpy
  ¹/₈  teaspoon salt
  ¹/₂  cup semisweet chocolate morsels

1. Preheat the oven to 325°F.
2. Grease and flour an 8" square baking pan.
3. In a large bowl, cream the butter or margarine with the sugar until the sugar is fully incorporated. Beat in the egg, then the vanilla.
4. In another bowl, stir together the flour, cornstarch, cocoa, and salt. Add to the creamed mixture, stirring until the dry ingredients are incorporated.
5. Spread the batter evenly in the prepared pan.

Bake the shortbread for 30 minutes or until a toothpick inserted in the center comes out clean.

6. Remove the pan from the oven, and turn the oven off. Immediately sprinkle the chocolate over the shortbread. Return the pan to the turned-off oven for 5 minutes. Remove the pan, and use a knife to spread the melted chocolate evenly over the shortbread. Transfer the pan to a rack to cool. When cool, cut into squares.

*Preparation time: 25 minutes*
*Yield: 16 squares*

# Cookie Snow Caps

These bars contain a cookie base topped with a sweet, rich filling that includes chopped nuts and Sno•Caps (these look like chocolate chips covered with hard white candy dots, which add a pleasing crunchiness). Kids especially love these bars.

## COOKIE LAYER

- 1 stick ($\frac{1}{2}$ cup) butter or margarine, softened
- $\frac{1}{2}$ cup brown sugar, preferably dark
- 1 teaspoon milk
- $\frac{1}{2}$ teaspoon vanilla
- 1 cup flour
- $\frac{1}{2}$ cup whole-wheat flour
- $\frac{1}{8}$ teaspoon salt
- $\frac{1}{2}$ cup finely chopped walnuts

## FILLING

- 2 eggs
- $\frac{1}{4}$ cup sugar
- $\frac{1}{2}$ cup brown sugar, preferably dark
- $\frac{1}{4}$ cup honey
- 1 teaspoon vanilla
- $\frac{1}{4}$ teaspoon salt
- $1\frac{1}{2}$ cups chopped walnuts
- 1 cup Sno•Caps candies

1. Preheat the oven to 350°F.
2. Grease and flour a 9" x 13" baking pan.

3. To make the cookie layer, in a large bowl, cream the butter or margarine with the brown sugar until the sugar is fully incorporated. Beat in the milk and vanilla.

4. In another bowl, stir together the flour, whole-wheat flour, and salt. Add to the creamed mixture, stirring until the dry ingredients are incorporated. Stir in the walnuts.

5. Pat the dough evenly in the prepared pan. Bake the cookie layer for 20 minutes.

6. Meanwhile, prepare the filling. In a bowl, beat the eggs. Gradually beat in the sugar, brown sugar, and honey until the mixture is thick. Stir in the vanilla, salt, walnuts, and Sno•Caps.

7. When the cookie layer has finished baking, pour the filling evenly over it. Bake the cake 30 minutes longer or until the filling is set and firm to the touch. Transfer the pan to a rack to cool. When cool, cut into bars.

***Preparation time: 25 minutes***
***Yield: 32 bars***

# Fudge-Filled Blondies

Considering how addicted I am to cake, it's not surprising that I frequently diet — although my definition of diet means limiting myself to a single piece of cake a day (omitting cake altogether would amount to total deprivation). At any rate, during one of my many diets, I sampled these delicious bars at a party and, in a highly disciplined manner, ate only one, although I could have easily eaten the whole plateful. Knowing I'd want another bar or two at a future date, I requested the recipe from the person who contributed them to the party. She promised to send it to me but, alas, never did. After much experimentation, I finally duplicated these wonderful, chewy "blond" brownies, filled with a layer of fudge.

|   | |
|---|---|
| 2 | sticks (1 cup) butter or margarine, softened (try to use at least half butter) |
| 1 | cup sugar |
| $^2/_3$ | cup brown sugar, preferably dark |
| 2 | eggs |
| 2 | teaspoons vanilla |
| $2^1/_2$ | cups flour |
| 1 | teaspoon baking soda |
| $^1/_4$ | teaspoon salt |
| 12 | ounces semisweet chocolate, melted |
| 1 | can sweetened condensed milk (not evaporated milk) |

1. Preheat the oven to 375°F.
2. Grease and flour a 9" x 13" baking pan.
3. In a large bowl, cream the butter or margarine with the sugar and brown sugar until the sugars are fully incorporated. Beat in the eggs, then the vanilla.
4. In another bowl, stir together the flour, baking soda, and salt. Add to the creamed mixture, stirring until the dry ingredients are incorporated.
5. Spread half the batter evenly in the prepared pan. Stir together the melted chocolate and condensed milk. Spread over the batter in an even layer. Cover with the remaining batter. The easiest way to do this is to drop little mounds of batter over the top of the filling. Then, using your fingertips, pinch the pieces together until they make a fairly even layer. You will not be able to cover the chocolate completely.
6. Bake the bars for 25 minutes or until a toothpick inserted in the center comes out clean. Transfer the pan to a rack to cool. When cool, cut into bars.

*Preparation time: 25 minutes*
*Yield: 30 blondies*

# Chocolate Chip–Oatmeal Blondies

There are certain foods that everyone seems to love and no one ever tires of. Oatmeal blondies with chocolate chips are one of these. The combination of oats and whole-wheat flour makes them especially hearty. They're a good choice for shipping.

       2  **sticks (1 cup) butter or margarine, softened**
    2¼  **cups brown sugar, preferably dark**
       2  **eggs**
     ½  **cup water**
    1¼  **cups flour**
       1  **cup whole-wheat flour**
       4  **cups rolled oats**
       1  **tablespoon baking powder**
     ¼  **teaspoon salt**
    1⅔  **cups (about 10 ounces) semisweet chocolate morsels**

1. Preheat the oven to 375°F.
2. Grease and flour a 9" square baking pan.
3. In a large bowl, cream the butter or margarine and brown sugar until the sugar is fully incorporated. Beat in the eggs, then the water.
4. In another bowl, stir together the flour, whole-wheat flour, oats, baking powder, and salt. Add to the creamed mixture, stirring until the dry ingredients are incorporated. Stir in the

chocolate chips. (The batter will be very stiff.)
5. Spread the batter evenly in the prepared pan. Bake the blondies for 30 minutes or until a toothpick inserted in the center comes out clean. Transfer the pan to a rack to cool. When cool, cut into bars.

*Preparation time: 25 minutes*
*Yield: 25 to 30 blondies*

# "Turtle"-Topped Oat Bars

In case you're unfamiliar with "turtles," these are candies made from pecans that are held together with caramel. The tops are then dunked into dark chocolate, so the result looks like a little turtle. The name "turtle" has come to refer to any dessert that combines pecans, chocolate, and caramel. The bottom layer of these bars is like a hearty oatmeal cookie, while the "turtle" topping is bound to be everyone's favorite.

## BOTTOM LAYER
- 1³/₄ cups rolled oats
- ³/₄ cup flour
- ³/₄ cup whole-wheat flour
- ³/₄ cup brown sugar, preferably dark
- ¹/₈ teaspoon salt
- 1¹/₂ sticks (³/₄ cup) butter or margarine, melted

## "TURTLE" LAYER
- 1 cup chopped pecans
- 1 6-ounce package semisweet chocolate morsels
- 1 12.6-ounce jar caramel or butterscotch ice-cream topping
- ¹/₄ cup flour

1. Preheat the oven to 350°F.
2. Grease and flour a 9" X 13" baking pan.

3. To make the bottom layer, in a large bowl, stir together all the bottom-layer ingredients. Reserve 1 cup for later use. Pat the rest of the mixture evenly into the bottom of the prepared pan.
4. Bake the bottom layer 10 minutes.
5. Remove the baking pan from the oven. Sprinkle with the pecans and chocolate. Stir together the ice-cream topping and flour, and drizzle this over the top. Sprinkle with the reserved mixture from the bottom layer. Return the pan to the oven, and bake 20 minutes longer or until the topping is lightly browned. Transfer the pan to a rack to cool. When cool, cut into bars.

*Preparation time: 20 minutes*
*Yield: 24 bars*

# Two-Layer Cookie Bars

The bottom layer of these cookie bars is rich and buttery — a great contrast to the many crunchy almonds in the candy-like topping.

## TOPPING
- 10²/₃ tablespoons (²/₃ cup) butter or margarine, melted
- 2 cups chopped almonds
- ¹/₂ cup sugar
- ¹/₄ cup honey
- ¹/₂ cup brandy
- 1 ¹/₂ teaspoons almond extract

## BOTTOM LAYER
- 2 sticks (1 cup) butter or margarine, softened
- 1 cup sugar
- 2 eggs
- 3¹/₂ cups flour
- ¹/₄ teaspoon salt

1. To make the topping, in a bowl, mix together all the topping ingredients. Set aside.
2. Preheat the oven to 350°F.
3. Grease and flour an 11" x 16" jelly roll pan.
4. To make the bottom layer, in a large bowl, cream the butter or margarine with the sugar until the sugar is fully incorporated. Beat in the eggs.

5. In another bowl, stir together the flour and salt. Add to the creamed mixture, stirring until the dry ingredients are incorporated.
6. Using your fingertips, pat the bottom layer evenly in the prepared pan. Spread the topping mixture evenly over the bottom layer.
7. Bake the bars for 25 minutes or until the topping is browned and set. Transfer the pan to a rack to cool. When cool, cut into bars.

*Preparation time: 20 minutes*
*Yield: 40 bars*

# "Trail Mix" Squares

These bars — containing whole-wheat flour, wheat germ, nuts, and dried fruits — have a hearty, wholesome appeal. This combination of ingredients makes these bars taste very much like the popular "trail mix" snack.

*Note:* For the raisins, prunes, and figs, you may substitute other dried fruits of your choice.

## BOTTOM LAYER
- $1/3$ cup honey
- $1/3$ cup vegetable oil
- $1/2$ cup flour
- $1/2$ cup whole-wheat flour
- $1/2$ cup wheat germ (not sweetened)
- 2 teaspoons baking powder

## TOP LAYER
- 2 eggs, well beaten
- $1/2$ cup chopped walnuts
- 1 cup shredded, sweetened coconut
- $1/4$ cup raisins
- $1/4$ cup chopped prunes
- $1/4$ cup chopped dried figs

1. Preheat the oven to 350°F.
2. Grease and flour an 8" square baking pan.
3. To make the bottom layer, beat the honey with the oil.
4. In another bowl, stir together the flour, whole-

wheat flour, wheat germ, and baking powder. Add to the honey mixture, stirring until the dry ingredients are incorporated.

5. Pat this mixture evenly into the bottom of the prepared pan. Bake the bottom layer for 10 minutes.

6. Meanwhile, prepare the top layer. In a bowl, mix together all the top-layer ingredients. Pour over the bottom layer, and bake 25 minutes longer or until the top is set and lightly browned. Transfer the pan to a rack to cool. When cool, cut into squares.

*Preparation time: 25 minutes*
*Yield: 16 squares*

# Granola Bars

Since granola-type cereals contain a wide variety of grains, nuts, and dried fruits, they easily add several different flavors and textures to a "blondie" bar. This is a very quick recipe to prepare.

1 stick ($\frac{1}{2}$ cup) butter or margarine, softened
$\frac{3}{4}$ cup brown sugar, preferably dark
1 egg
2 tablespoons milk
$\frac{1}{2}$ cup flour
$\frac{1}{2}$ cup whole-wheat flour
1 teaspoon baking powder
2 cups granola or similar cereal

1. Preheat the oven to 350°F.
2. Grease and flour a 9" x 13" baking pan.
3. In a large bowl, cream the butter or margarine with the sugar until the sugar is fully incorporated. Beat in the egg, then the milk.
4. In another bowl, stir together the flour, whole-wheat flour, and baking powder. Add to the creamed mixture, stirring until the dry ingredients are incorporated. Stir in the granola.
5. Spread the batter evenly in the prepared pan. Bake the bars for 30 minutes or until a toothpick inserted in the center comes out clean. Transfer the pan to a rack to cool. When cool, cut into bars.

*Preparation time: 15 minutes*
*Yield: 15 bars*

# Honey-Almond Fruit Bars

These bars are ideal for gift giving, especially during the holiday season. They keep well, so they are a particularly good choice for shipping. Almost any dried fruits are delicious in these bars. I use a mixture of raisins, dried figs, dates, dried apricots, prunes, and dried pineapple.

   2  eggs
  ²/₃  cup sugar
  ¹/₂  cup honey
   1  stick (¹/₂ cup) butter or margarine, melted
 1¹/₂  cups flour
 1¹/₂  cups whole-wheat flour
 1¹/₂  teaspoons baking powder
   1  teaspoon baking soda
   1  teaspoon cinnamon
  ¹/₂  teaspoon nutmeg
  ¹/₄  teaspoon ground cloves
  ¹/₈  teaspoon salt
   1  cup finely ground almonds
 1¹/₂  cups dried fruits of your choice, chopped

1. Preheat the oven to 350°F.
2. Grease and flour a 9" x 13" baking pan.
3. In a large bowl, beat the eggs. Beat in the sugar and honey gradually until the mixture is thick. Beat in the melted butter or margarine.

4. In another bowl, stir together the flour, whole-wheat flour, baking powder, baking soda, cinnamon, nutmeg, cloves, salt, and ground almonds. Add to the honey mixture, stirring until the dry ingredients are incorporated. Stir in the dried fruits. The batter will be very stiff, so you may wish to use your hands for this.
5. Pat the batter evenly in the prepared pan. (It's easiest to use your hands; lightly flour them first so that the batter doesn't stick to your fingers.) Bake the bars for 30 minutes or until a toothpick inserted in the center comes out clean. Transfer the pan to a rack to cool. When cool, cut into bars.

*Preparation time: 30 minutes*
*Yield: 32 bars*

# Walnut Bars

These easy-to-make bars are very attractive because they're spread with beaten egg whites and sprinkled with nuts before baking. The result is a crispy, browned bar.

1½ **sticks (¾ cup) butter or margarine, softened**
1 **cup brown sugar, preferably dark**
2 **eggs, separated**
1 **teaspoon vanilla**
2 **cups flour**
1 **teaspoon baking powder**
1 **teaspoon cinnamon**
½ **teaspoon nutmeg**
¼ **teaspoon salt**
1 **cup finely chopped walnuts**

1. Preheat the oven to 350°F.
2. Grease and flour a 9" x 13" baking pan.
3. In a large bowl, cream the butter or margarine with the sugar until the sugar is fully incorporated. Beat in the egg yolks, then the vanilla.
4. In another bowl, stir together the flour, baking powder, cinnamon, nutmeg, and salt. Add to the creamed mixture, stirring until the dry ingredients are incorporated.
5. Spread the batter evenly in the prepared pan. Using a fork, beat the egg whites in a small bowl just until frothy. Spread over the dough

and sprinkle with the walnuts.

6. Bake the bars for 25 minutes or until a toothpick inserted in the center comes out clean. Transfer the pan to a rack to cool. When cool, cut into bars.

*Preparation time: 25 minutes*
*Yield: 18 bars*

# Crumb-Topped Raisin Bars

Lots of butter and sour cream make these raisin bars incredibly rich. With a crust like a crunchy oatmeal cookie, the filling a lovely raisin-studded custard, and more of the oat crust sprinkled on top, these are very special bars, indeed.

*Note:* These bars should be kept refrigerated and, in fact, are better cold than at room temperature. Also, unlike most bars, these are best eaten with a fork.

## CRUST AND TOPPING

- 2 sticks (1 cup) butter or margarine, softened (try to use at least half butter)
- 1 cup brown sugar, preferably dark
- 1³/₄ cups rolled oats
- 1³/₄ cups flour
- 1 teaspoon baking soda

## FILLING

- 1¹/₂ cups boiling water
- 2 cups raisins
- 3 eggs
- 1¹/₂ cups sour cream
- 1 cup sugar
- 2¹/₂ tablespoons cornstarch
- 1 tablespoon vanilla

1. Preheat the oven to 350°F.
2. Grease and flour a 9" x 13" baking pan.
3. To make the crust and topping, in a large bowl, cream the butter or margarine with the brown sugar until the sugar is fully incorporated. Beat in the oats, flour, and baking soda. The mixture will be crumbly.
4. Pat half the oat mixture into the prepared pan, and reserve the remaining mixture. Bake the crust for 7 minutes.
5. Meanwhile, prepare the filling. Pour the boiling water over the raisins. Let sit for 5 minutes. Drain the raisins well, discarding the soaking liquid.
6. In a heavy saucepan, combine the eggs, sour cream, sugar, and cornstarch. Cook over a low heat, stirring, until the mixture is thick. Remove from the heat, and stir in the raisins and vanilla. Spread over the oat crust.
7. Sprinkle the remaining oat mixture evenly over the raisin custard.
8. Return the pan to the hot oven. Bake the bars for 30 minutes. Transfer the pan to a rack to cool. When cool, refrigerate the bars until firm. When cold, cut into bars.

*Preparation time: 30 minutes*
*Yield: 32 bars*

# Pineapple Scotchies

These are similar to traditional date bars, but the crumbly oat crust is filled with a sweet pineapple mixture instead.

**FILLING**

  1 **16-ounce can crushed pineapple, preferably packed in juice, drained**
  $^1/_4$ **cup sugar**
  3 **tablespoons orange marmalade**
  1 **tablespoon cornstarch**

**BARS**

  $1^1/_2$ **sticks ($^3/_4$ cup) butter or margarine, softened**
  1 **cup brown sugar, preferably dark**
  $1^1/_2$ **cups flour**
  $1^1/_2$ **cups rolled oats**
  $^1/_2$ **teaspoon baking soda**

1. To make the filling, in a small, heavy saucepan, combine all the filling ingredients. Bring to a full boil, stirring constantly. Remove from the heat, and set aside.
2. Preheat the oven to 375°F.
3. Grease and flour a 9" square baking pan.
4. To make the bars, in a large bowl, mix together all the bar ingredients until crumbly.
5. Pour half the bar mixture into the prepared pan. Press down firmly with your fingertips to

make a crust. Spread the pineapple filling evenly over the crust. Sprinkle with the remaining bar mixture, and press down lightly with your fingertips.

6. Bake the bars for 40 minutes or until golden. Transfer the pan to a rack to cool. When cool, cut into bars.

*Preparation time: 20 minutes*
*Yield: 16 scotchies*

# CHAPTER NINE

# SPECIAL-OCCASION CAKES

Most recipes in this cookbook are intended to provide, if not instant gratification, at least pleasure that comes quickly and easily. This is why I've selected cakes that not only can generally be prepared in 30 minutes or less, but are so flavorful on their own that they need no icing. Many can even be enjoyed warm from the oven.

However, among the recipes I frequently prepare are favorites that don't fit into any other chapter of the book. Although some of these cakes take more than 30 minutes to prepare, I wanted to share them with other bakers who love cake as much as I do.

Thus, in this chapter, you'll find ideas for children's birthday cakes, an outrageous cheesecake, a fabulous ice cream cake, and a blueberry "pizza" brunch cake. You may not even want to wait for a special occasion to try these recipes.

# Brownie–Ice Cream Fudge Cake

From the time I was a child, it was my responsibility to prepare the dessert for Thanksgiving dinner. Since neither my family nor I much liked pumpkin pie, I simply made a different festive dessert each year. However my family is inordinately fond of ice cream, so eventually I began making ice cream cakes. I tested out different versions until I hit upon this one, which was immediately awarded a "10"; I've made it every year since. In fact, my daughter, who remembers no other Thanksgiving dessert, regards this as the traditional ending to a Thanksgiving meal. Although we reserve this ice cream cake for our Thanksgiving holiday, there's no reason why you shouldn't serve it for any special occasion. The cake is very easy to put together and can be assembled in advance.

## CRUST
- 17 **Oreo cookies, crushed**
- 3 **tablespoons butter or margarine, melted**

## FILLING
- 1 **recipe World's Best Brownies, without the topping (page 252)**
- 3 **pints premium vanilla ice cream, softened slightly**

# FUDGE SAUCE

 4 1-ounce squares unsweetened
 chocolate
 1 cup sugar
 1/8 teaspoon salt
 1 tablespoon butter or margarine
 1 cup light cream or half-and-half
 1/2 teaspoon vanilla

1. Preheat the oven to 325°F.
2. To make the crust, mix together the crushed Oreos and melted butter or margarine. Press into the bottom of a 9" square baking pan. Bake the crust for 10 minutes. Remove from the oven, and cool to room temperature.
3. To make the filling, make one recipe of the World's Best Brownies. When the brownies have cooled, cut them into squares, about 1/2" X 1/2".
4. To assemble the cake, spoon half the ice cream into the crust. Sprinkle with half the brownie cubes. Repeat the layers. Cover the cake with plastic wrap, and freeze for at least 3 hours.
5. Meanwhile, make the fudge sauce. In a large, heavy saucepan, melt the chocolate. Add the sugar, salt, butter or margarine, and cream or half-and-half. Cook over a low heat, stirring, for 5 minutes. Do not let the mixture come to a boil. Remove the pan from the heat, and stir in the vanilla. If not serving immediately, chill the sauce, and reheat before using.

6. To serve the ice cream cake, put a generous square of cake on each plate, and cover with a generous serving of fudge sauce.

*Preparation time:*
   *Crust — 10 minutes*
   *Filling — 20 minutes to prepare,*
      *10 minutes to assemble with*
      *ice cream*
   *Sauce — 10 minutes*
*Yield: 12 servings*

# Mini Surprise Cupcakes

These are great for a child's party. (When my daughter brought them to school on her birthday, everyone in her class loved them.) The cupcakes are very easy to make, and cleanup is much faster if you line the tins with foil or paper muffin liners. If you wish, frost with Chocolate Butter Frosting (page 339) or Vanilla Frosting (page 340).

 1  **stick (¹/₂ cup) butter or margarine, softened**
 1  **cup sugar**
 3  **eggs**
 ³/₄  **cup milk**
 1  **teaspoon vanilla**
 2  **cups minus 2 tablespoons flour**
 2  **teaspoons baking powder**
 ¹/₄  **teaspoon salt**
 ¹/₂  **cup assorted candies, such as M&M's, Hershey's Kisses, cut-up 3 Musketeers candy bars, chocolate chips, and so forth**

1. Preheat the oven to 375°F.
2. Line 36 mini-muffin tins with liners. Or grease and flour the tins. If you do not have enough muffin pans, you will need to make the cupcakes in two or three batches.
3. In a large bowl, cream the butter or margarine with the sugar until the sugar is fully incorpo-

rated. Beat in the eggs, then the milk and vanilla.

4. In another bowl, stir together the flour, baking powder, and salt. Add to the creamed mixture, stirring until the dry ingredients are incorporated. Stir in the candies.

5. Fill each muffin tin nearly to the top with the batter. Make certain that at least one piece of candy goes into each tin.

6. Bake the cupcakes for 12 to 15 minutes or until a toothpick inserted in the center of a cupcake comes out clean. Transfer the pan to a rack to cool. When fully cool, frost the cupcakes (if desired).

*Preparation time: 25 minutes*
*Yield: 36 mini-cupcakes*

# "Pizza" Cake

"Pizza" Cake is really a giant chocolate chip cookie, decorated to look like a pizza. It's great for a child's birthday party, but is equally popular with adults. Serve it for dessert at an informal buffet or Super Bowl party.

## CAKE
- 1½ sticks (¾ cup) butter or margarine, softened
- ¾ cup sugar
- ½ cup brown sugar, preferably dark
- 2 eggs
- 1½ teaspoons vanilla
- 1⅔ cups flour
- ½ teaspoon baking soda
- ⅛ teaspoon salt
- ¾ cup semisweet chocolate morsels, ground in a food processor so that some become powdery and the rest remain in small chunks

## TOPPINGS
- ⅔ cup seedless red jam, such as strawberry (or use vanilla frosting, tinted a very dark pink)
- 2 regular-size Tootsie Rolls, cut into ¼-inch slices
- 4 ounces white chocolate

1. Preheat the oven to 375°F.
2. Grease and flour a 13" round pizza pan.
3. To make the cake, in a large bowl, cream the butter or margarine with the sugar and brown sugar until the sugars are fully incorporated. Beat in the eggs, then the vanilla.
4. In another bowl, stir together the flour, baking soda, and salt. Add to the creamed mixture, stirring until the dry ingredients are incorporated. Stir in the chocolate.
5. Using lightly floured hands, pat the dough evenly in the prepared pan. Do not make a rim of dough around the edge (as you would for a real pizza) since it will rise and overflow off the rim of the pan.
6. Place an upside down muffin tin (or something similar) on the oven rack so that when the "pizza," which has been placed on top of the tin, is ready to be taken out of the oven, you will be able to lift it by holding the bottom of the pan. It is important that you do not touch the outer crust of the "pizza" since it will be very soft and will most likely break off. (Once the cookie hardens to room temperature, however, it will be less fragile.)
7. Bake the pizza for 20 minutes or until a toothpick inserted in the center comes out clean. Transfer the pan to a rack to cool.
8. When completely cooled, add the toppings. Spread the jam or frosting over the "pizza," leaving about 1" of crust showing around the edges. Shape the Tootsie Roll slices into

rounds, and scatter them over the top of the pizza like you would sausage slices.

9. Very carefully melt the white chocolate (which burns more easily than dark chocolate). Drizzle over the pizza as "cheese."

*Preparation time: 30 minutes*
*Yield: 16 to 20 "slices"*

# Teddy Bear Cake

This is an easily made, adorable cake for a young child's birthday party. Teddy Graham sandwich cookies are embedded in a delicious butter batter, and additional Teddy Grahams decorate the frosted cake.

## CAKE

- 2 sticks (1 cup) butter or margarine, softened (try to use at least half butter)
- 1$\frac{1}{2}$ cups sugar
- 4 eggs
- 1$\frac{1}{4}$ cups milk
- 1 teaspoon vanilla
- 3 cups flour
- 2$\frac{1}{2}$ teaspoons baking powder
- $\frac{1}{8}$ teaspoon salt
- 50 vanilla-filled chocolate Teddy Graham sandwich cookies

## TOPPING

- 1 recipe Creamy White Icing (page 334)
  About 25 Teddy Graham cookies (not sandwich) in assorted flavors, if desired

1. Preheat the oven to 350°F.
2. Grease and flour a tube pan.

3. To make the cake, in a large bowl, cream the butter or margarine with the sugar until the sugar is fully incorporated. Beat in the eggs, then the milk and vanilla.
4. In another bowl, stir together the flour, baking powder, and salt. Add to the creamed mixture, stirring until the dry ingredients are incorporated. Stir in the Teddy Graham sandwich cookies.
5. Turn the batter out into the prepared pan. Bake the cake for 1 hour or until a toothpick inserted in the highest part of the cake comes out clean. Transfer the pan to a rack to cool.
6. When completely cool, remove the cake from the pan and frost with the Creamy White Icing. Scatter Teddy Grahams over the top and sides of the cake. Press on the cookies lightly so that they stick to the icing.

*Preparation time: 20 minutes*
*Yield: 16 to 20 servings*

# Blueberry Pizza

This recipe starts with a pizza crust, which is then spread with a luscious ricotta cheese filling and topped with fresh blueberries. Served warm from the oven, this is one of the best blueberry coffee cakes imaginable.

*Note:* I have an automatic bread machine, so I just place all the ingredients for the dough in the container, push a button, and, 2 hours later, I have perfect pizza dough. I realize that not everyone owns this kitchen wonder, so the dough can be made by hand with just a little more effort.

## DOUGH
- $^2/_3$ cup warm water
- $^1/_2$ cup whole-wheat flour
- 1 teaspoon salt
- 1 teaspoon sugar
- 2 tablespoons vegetable oil
- 2 teaspoons yeast
- $1^1/_2$ cups bread flour

## TOPPING
- $^7/_8$ cup ricotta
- 3 tablespoons amaretto liqueur
- 3 tablespoons orange liqueur
- 1 pint blueberries, washed and picked over
- 6 tablespoons sugar

1. To make the dough, use a bread machine, following the manufacturer's instructions. Or, to make the dough by hand, in a large bowl, stir together the water, whole-wheat flour, salt, sugar, oil, and yeast. Gradually stir in the bread flour. Knead the dough until smooth. Then place the dough in a greased bowl, cover the bowl, and let the dough sit in a warm place for about 1 hour to rise.
2. Meanwhile, make the topping. Stir together the ricotta, amaretto, and orange liqueur. Set aside.
3. Preheat the oven to 375°F.
4. Grease and flour a 13" round pizza pan.
5. Stretch the dough to fit in the prepared pan, pushing the dough up on the rim.
6. Spread the ricotta mixture over the dough, leaving a ½" border all around. sprinkle with the blueberries, then the sugar.
7. Bake the pizza for 30 minutes or until the crust is browned. Serve warm from the oven.

*Preparation time: 20 minutes*
  *plus rising time and baking time*
*Yield: 6 to 8 servings*

# The Flowerpot

This cake looks so much like a real flowerpot, you can use it as the centerpiece for your table. It will take a while for the guests to realize it's edible. It makes a perfect cake for a young girl's birthday or for a Sweet Sixteen party or for such holidays as Valentine's Day, Easter and Mother's Day.

Although the cake looks spectacular, it is very easy to prepare. It is baked in a deep mixing bowl to give it the shape of a flowerpot. The bowl I use measures 4" on the bottom, 8" across the top, and $5^{1}/_{2}$" high. Any bowl of similar proportions will work well.

After baking, the cake is covered with terra-cotta–colored icing and decorated with candies to emphasize the flowerpot shape. The top is sprinkled with crushed Oreo cookies (to resemble "dirt"). As the final touch, I insert three long-stemmed white chocolate roses into the top of the cake, and the effect is complete. In candy shops, I have been able to find white chocolate roses colored white, pink, and red and prefer to use one of each color for the cake. You may use all of one color, if you wish. Another option is to use milk chocolate roses that have been wrapped in red foil.

Not only is this lovely to look at, but it also tastes wonderful. The cake starts with a rich, sour cream–butter batter. A mixture of chocolate syrup and melted chocolate candies is added to half the batter, and the two batters are marbleized. I've never met anyone who didn't love this cake.

# CAKE

 2 sticks (1 cup) butter or margarine, softened (try to use at least half butter)
 2 cups sugar
 5 eggs
 1 teaspoon vanilla
 1½ cups sour cream
 2½ cups flour
 1 teaspoon baking soda
 ¼ teaspoon salt
 1 14-ounce package Hershey's Assorted Chocolate Miniatures
 ½ cup Hershey's Chocolate Syrup

1. Preheat the oven to 350°F.
2. Grease and flour a large, deep mixing bowl.
3. To make the cake, in a large bowl, cream the butter or margarine with the sugar until the sugar is fully incorporated. Beat in the eggs, then the vanilla and sour cream.
4. In another bowl, stir together the flour, baking soda, and salt. Add to the creamed mixture, stirring until the dry ingredients are incorporated.
5. In a small saucepan, melt the chocolate candies in the chocolate syrup.
6. Transfer half the batter to another bowl, and stir in the chocolate mixture.

# FROSTING AND DECORATION

   2 recipes Vanilla Frosting (page 340)
   Red and yellow food coloring
   About 2 teaspoons unsweetened
      cocoa powder (for coloring)
   About 80 small candies such as
      Smarties, Skittles, or M&M's
  10 Oreo cookies, crushed
   3 long-stemmed white chocolate roses

7. Drop large spoonfuls of the white and chocolate batters alternately into the prepared bowl.
   Swirl the two batters with a knife to create a
   marbleized effect.
8. Bake the cake for 45 minutes. Then lower the
   oven temperature to 325°F, and bake 1 hour
   longer or until a long knife inserted in the
   center comes out clean.
9. Transfer the bowl to a rack to cool. When
   cool, remove the cake from the bowl, and
   place it, right side up, on a serving plate. Let
   it cool completely before frosting it.
10. To make the frosting and decorations, tint
   the vanilla frosting pale orange, using the red
   and yellow food coloring. (You will need
   about 3 times as many drops of yellow food
   coloring as red.) Then, using cocoa powder,
   continue to tint the frosting until it resembles
   terra-cotta. Cover the cake completely with
   the icing.
11. About 1" down from the top rim of the cake,
   make two rows of small candies. This will look

like the border of a real flower pot. Leaving ½" space around the perimeter of the cake, sprinkle the top of the cake with the crushed Oreos. Insert the roses into the center of the cake.

*Preparation time: 30 minutes to mix the batter plus 30 minutes to make the frosting and decorate the cake*
*Yield: 20 servings*

# Heath Bar Cheesecake

At a country inn in Pennsylvania, I sampled a Heath Bar cheesecake and knew that I would feel sorely deprived if that single slice were to constitute my lifetime's allotment. Thus, I resolved to recreate the recipe in my own kitchen, and I think all cheesecake fans would agree that the results are nothing short of fabulous. As everyone knows, cheesecake is a true indulgence dessert, and this recipe is no exception, with an Oreo cookie crust and a filling that contains a plentiful helping of chopped Heath bars, 4 packages of cream cheese, and 7 egg yolks. But the taste is pure heaven!

*Note:* This cake should be stored in the refrigerator.

## CRUST
   25  **Oreo cookies, coarsely crushed**
   ¹/₂  **stick (4 tablespoons) butter or margarine, melted**

## FILLING
   4  **8-ounce packages cream cheese, softened**
  1¹/₄  **cups sugar**
   2  **tablespoons flour**
   4  **eggs**
   3  **egg yolks**
   ¹/₃  **cup heavy cream or whipping cream**
   1  **teaspoon vanilla**
  1¹/₄  **cups plus ¹/₄ cup chopped Heath**

## bars, divided usage

1. Grease a 9" x 13" baking pan.
2. To make the crust, mix together the crushed Oreos and melted butter. Press evenly into the bottom of the prepared pan. Chill while preparing the filling.
3. Preheat the oven to 425°F.
4. To make the filling, in a large bowl, cream the cream cheese with the sugar until the sugar is fully incorporated. Beat in the flour, whole eggs, and egg yolks until the mixture is smooth. Beat in the cream and vanilla.
5. Sprinkle the 1¼ cups of chopped Heath bars evenly over the crust. Pour the filling into the pan.
6. Bake the cheesecake for 15 minutes. Then lower the oven temperature to 225°F, and continue baking 50 minutes longer or until the cheesecake is set. Transfer the pan to a rack to cool, and immediately sprinkle with the ¼ cup of chopped Heath Bars.
7. When cooled to room temperature, place the cheesecake in the refrigerator, and chill for several hours before serving.

*Preparation time: 30 minutes*
*Yield: 25 servings*

# CHAPTER TEN

# BONUS CAKE RECIPES

Like most cooks, I have my favorite cookbooks as well as my favorite recipes within those books. These are the recipes I prepare again and again, finding comfort in their familiarity and in the knowledge that whenever I make them, they'll be as delicious as the time before.

After *The Good Cake Book* was published, I began using it as I do any favorite cookbook. Thus, the pages have become rather "dog-eared," and the book falls open to those recipes that I make repeatedly. Some of these recipes are included here. I hope you enjoy them as much as my family and I do.

# Grandmother's Jam Squares

My grandmother was a decidedly unadventuresome cook. The few recipes she found that she liked, she made again and again for years on end. Unfortunately, most of these are not worth passing along. But this recipe and the following one for date and nut bread should most definitely be recorded for posterity. These jam squares are in two layers: a rich, butter-and-egg-yolk base is spread with jam and then topped with a light meringue.

*Note:* Use any jam; strawberry, apricot, and raspberry all work well.

## MERINGUE TOPPING
- 2 **egg whites**
- $^1/_2$ **cup sugar**
- $^1/_4$ **teaspoon cinnamon**
- $^1/_2$ **cup finely chopped walnuts**

## BASE
- 1 **stick ($^1/_2$ cup) butter or margarine, softened (try to use at least half butter)**
- $^1/_2$ **cup confectioners' sugar**
- 2 **egg yolks**
- 1 **cup flour**
- $^2/_3$ **cup jam (see *Note,* above)**

1. Preheat the oven to 350°F.
2. Grease and flour an 8" square baking pan.
3. To make the meringue topping, in a large bowl, beat the egg whites until stiff. Gradually beat in the sugar until the mixture is glossy. Beat in the cinnamon and walnuts and set aside.
4. To make the base, in another bowl, cream the butter or margarine with the confectioners' sugar until the sugar is fully incorporated. Beat in the egg yolks, then the flour.
5. Pat the dough evenly in the prepared pan. Bake for 12 minutes.
6. Remove the pan from the oven, and spread the jam evenly over the base layer. Spread the meringue topping over the jam. Return the pan to the oven, and bake 20 minutes longer. Transfer the pan to a rack to cool. When cool, cut into squares.

*Preparation time: 20 minutes*
*Yield: 25 squares*

# Grandmother's Date and Nut Bread

My grandmother always made this recipe in two-loaf batches because it was so popular. The bread (which is really more of a tea cake) has an excellent date flavor since the liquid used to soften the dates goes into the batter. The bread is delicious as a not-too-sweet dessert or between-meal snack, or, spread with cream cheese, used for delicate sandwiches. It ships very well.

| | |
|---|---|
| 1 | 8-ounce package chopped pitted dates |
| ½ | cup raisins |
| 3 | tablespoons butter or margarine, softened |
| 2 | teaspoons baking soda |
| 2 | teaspoons instant coffee powder |
| 2 | cups boiling water |
| 2 | eggs |
| 1½ | cups sugar |
| 1 | teaspoon vanilla |
| 3 | cups flour |
| 1 | cup whole-wheat flour |
| ½ | teaspoon cinnamon |
| 1 | cup coarsely chopped walnuts |

1. To a large bowl, add the dates, raisins, butter or margarine, baking soda, coffee powder, and boiling water. Let sit until lukewarm, stirring

occasionally. Then drain, reserving the liquid.

2. Preheat the oven to 350°F.
3. Grease and flour two loaf pans, each 9" x 5".
4. In another large bowl, beat the eggs. Gradually beat in the sugar until the mixture is thick and pale yellow. Beat in the drained date liquid and the vanilla.
5. In a third bowl, stir together the flour, whole-wheat flour, and cinnamon. Add to the liquid mixture, stirring until the dry ingredients are incorporated. Stir in the reserved fruit mixture and the walnuts.
6. Divide the batter evenly between the two prepared pans. Bake the loaves for 1 hour or until a toothpick inserted in the center comes out clean. Transfer the loaves to a rack to cool.

*Preparation time: 25 minutes*
*Yield: 2 loaves, each yielding*
  *8 generous slices*

# Blueberry–Cream Cheese Cake

This is one of my husband's favorite cakes. The cake itself tastes like a luscious, sweet, crumbly blueberry muffin, and it's topped with a rich cream cheese filling that's covered with a delightful crumb mixture. As a coffee cake for breakfast or brunch, it's hard to find one more appealing than this. Or, for a summertime dessert, top each square of cake with a scoop of vanilla ice cream or frozen yogurt.

*Note:* Although there are three different mixtures to prepare for this cake, there's no need to wash the beaters between them. As another time-saving measure, you can prepare all three mixtures simultaneously. By this I mean that when you're measuring sugar for the cake batter, you can add the sugar to the bowl for the cream cheese filling and to the bowl for the crumb mixture. This cake should be stored in the refrigerator. For best flavor, bring the cake to room temperature before serving.

## CREAM CHEESE MIXTURE
   1   3-ounce package cream cheese, softened
   2   tablespoons sugar
   1   tablespoon lemon juice

## CRUMB TOPPING
   ¹/₂   cup flour
   ¹/₂   cup whole-wheat flour

    ¼  **cup sugar**
    2  **tablespoons butter or margarine,
        softened**
    ¼  **teaspoon cinnamon**

## CAKE

    5⅓  **tablespoons butter or margarine,
         softened**
    ⅓   **cup sugar**
    2   **eggs**
    ¾   **cup milk**
    ¾   **cup flour**
    ¾   **cup whole-wheat flour**
    1   **tablespoon baking powder**
    ¼   **teaspoon salt**
    2   **cups blueberries, divided usage**

1. To make the cream cheese mixture, in a bowl, place all the mixture ingredients, and mix well. Set aside.
2. To make the crumb topping, in another bowl, place all the topping ingredients, and mix until crumbly. Set aside.
3. Preheat the oven to 375°F.
4. Grease and flour an 8" x 10" baking pan.
5. To make the cake batter, in a large bowl, cream the butter or margarine with the sugar until the sugar is fully incorporated. Beat in the eggs, then the milk.
6. In another bowl, stir together the flour, whole-wheat flour, baking powder, and salt. Add to the creamed mixture, stirring until the dry in-

gredients are incorporated. Stir in half the blueberries.

7. Spread the batter evenly in the prepared pan. Sprinkle with the remaining blueberries. Drop tiny spoonfuls of the cream cheese mixture over the batter, and sprinkle with the crumb topping.

8. Bake the cake for 30 minutes or until a toothpick inserted in the center comes out clean. Transfer the pan to a rack to cool.

*Preparation time: 30 minutes*
*Yield: 12 servings*

# Chocolate-Zucchini Cake

For the first three years of my culinary career, I wrote a weekly newspaper column. Of all the recipes printed in these columns, this one, which appeared just when zucchini breads were coming into vogue, attracted the most attention and praise — praise because the shredded zucchini adds a wonderful texture to chocolate cakes, and attention because the cake is unusual and the name a conversation piece.

| | |
|---|---|
| 9 | tablespoons butter or margarine, softened |
| 2 | cups sugar |
| 3 | eggs |
| 3 | 1-ounce squares unsweetened chocolate, melted |
| 2 | teaspoons vanilla |
| 2 | teaspoons grated orange rind |
| ½ | cup milk |
| 2 | cups coarsely shredded zucchini |
| 2½ | cups flour |
| 2½ | teaspoons baking powder |
| 1 | teaspoon baking soda |
| 1 | teaspoon cinnamon |
| ¼ | teaspoon salt |

1. Preheat the oven to 350°F.
2. Grease and flour a tube pan.
3. In a large bowl, cream the butter or margarine

with the sugar until the sugar is fully incorporated. Beat in the eggs, then the chocolate, vanilla, orange rind, and milk. Stir in the zucchini.

4. In another bowl, stir together the flour, baking powder, baking soda, cinnamon, and salt. Add to the zucchini mixture, stirring until the dry ingredients are incorporated.

5. Turn the batter out into the prepared pan. Bake the cake for 1 hour or until a toothpick inserted in the highest part of the cake comes out clean. Transfer the pan to a rack to cool.

*Preparation time: 25 minutes*
*Yield: 16 servings*

# Pumpkin–Chocolate Chip Cake

Here's a dramatic tube cake that's praised by everyone. The pumpkin and spices give it a lovely color, and the cake is chock full of nuts, raisins, and chocolate chips. This is a cake for festive occasions and is even more appealing with Creamy White Icing (page 334).

  4  eggs
  2  cups sugar
  2  sticks (1 cup) butter or margarine, melted
  1  1-pound can solid-pack pumpkin (not pumpkin-pie filling)
  1  cup flour
  1  cup whole-wheat flour
  2  teaspoons baking powder
  1  teaspoon baking soda
 1$\frac{1}{2}$  teaspoons cinnamon
  $\frac{1}{2}$  teaspoon ground cloves
  $\frac{1}{4}$  teaspoon nutmeg
  $\frac{1}{4}$  teaspoon ginger
  $\frac{1}{4}$  teaspoon salt
  2  cups bran cereal, such as All-Bran
  1  6-ounce package semisweet chocolate morsels
  $\frac{2}{3}$  cup coarsely chopped walnuts
  $\frac{2}{3}$  cup raisins

1. Preheat the oven to 350°F.
2. Grease and flour a tube pan.
3. In a large bowl, beat the eggs. Gradually beat in the sugar until the mixture is thick and pale yellow. Beat in the melted butter or margarine, then the pumpkin.
4. In another bowl, stir together the flour, whole-wheat flour, baking powder, baking soda, cinnamon, cloves, nutmeg, ginger, salt, and cereal. Add to the pumpkin mixture, stirring until the dry ingredients are incorporated. Stir in the chocolate, walnuts, and raisins.
5. Turn the batter out into the prepared pan. Bake the cake for 1 hour 10 minutes or until a toothpick inserted in the highest part of the cake comes out clean. Transfer the pan to a rack to cool.

*Preparation time: 25 minutes*
*Yield: 16 to 20 servings*

# Chocolate-Banana Cake

This chocolate cake is rich with the fruity taste of banana. In this and all other banana cakes, be certain to use very ripe bananas — the darker the skin of the bananas, the sweeter and more flavorful the cake. Chocolate–Sour Cream Icing (page 335) is a good topping for this cake.

|   | |
|---|---|
| 9 | tablespoons butter or margarine, softened |
| 1¼ | cups sugar |
| 2 | eggs |
| ½ | cup buttermilk or 1½ teaspoons vinegar in a measuring cup plus milk up to the ½-cup mark |
| 1 | cup mashed ripe bananas |
| 1 | cup flour |
| ½ | cup unsweetened cocoa powder, sifted if lumpy |
| 1 | teaspoon baking soda |
| ¼ | teaspoon salt |

1. Preheat the oven to 350°F.
2. Grease and flour an 8" x 10" baking pan.
3. In a large bowl, cream the butter or margarine with the sugar until the sugar is fully incorporated. Beat in the eggs, then the buttermilk and bananas.
4. In another bowl, stir together the flour, cocoa, baking soda, and salt. Add to the banana mix-

ture, stirring until the dry ingredients are incorporated.

5. Turn the batter out into the prepared pan. Bake the cake for 35 minutes or until a toothpick inserted in the center comes out clean. Transfer the pan to a rack to cool.

*Preparation time: 25 minutes*
*Yield: 8 to 10 servings*

# Chocolate Chip Cake

This is a cake for kids . . . or for adults who still eat like kids. The golden-yellow cake is flecked with ground chocolate chips and then topped with plenty more. Warm from the oven, this is a special treat.

 1   stick (½ cup) butter or margarine, softened
1½   cups sugar
 2   eggs
 ½   teaspoon instant coffee powder, dissolved in 2 teaspoons hot water
1¼   cups milk
2½   cups plus 2 tablespoons flour
2½   teaspoons baking powder
 ¼   teaspoon salt
 1   6-ounce package semisweet chocolate morsels, half of them finely chopped in a blender or food processor
 ¼   cup coarsely chopped walnuts

1. Preheat the oven to 350°F.
2. Grease and flour an 8" x 10" baking pan.
3. In a large bowl, cream the butter or margarine with the sugar until the sugar is fully incorporated. Beat in the eggs, then the coffee and milk.
4. In another bowl, stir together the flour, baking

powder, and salt. Add to the creamed mixture, stirring until the dry ingredients are incorporated. Stir in the 3 ounces of finely chopped chocolate.

5. Spread the batter evenly in the prepared pan. Sprinkle with the remaining chocolate morsels and the walnuts. Bake the cake for 40 minutes or until a toothpick inserted in the center comes out clean. Transfer the pan to a rack to cool.

*Preparation time: 20 minutes*
*Yield: 12 to 16 servings*

# Jam Cake

I have baked this spice cake with nearly every jam imaginable — raspberry, pineapple, fig, and strawberry, for example — and every time it has been delightful. You can also use marmalade in the recipe (but not jelly, which has a different consistency). Red jams lend a beautiful pink tint to the cake. This easy-to-prepare cake keeps and ships very well. It's also delicious spread with Creamy White Icing (page 334).

  6  **tablespoons butter or margarine, softened**
  1  **cup brown sugar, preferably dark**
  2  **eggs**
  3  **tablespoons sour cream**
  1  **cup jam (any flavor)**
1½  **cups flour**
  1  **teaspoon baking powder**
  ½  **teaspoon baking soda**
  1  **teaspoon cinnamon**
  1  **teaspoon nutmeg**
  ½  **teaspoon ground cloves**

1. Preheat the oven to 350°F.
2. Grease and flour a 9" x 5" loaf pan.
3. In a large bowl, cream the butter or margarine with the brown sugar until the sugar is fully incorporated. Beat in the eggs, then the sour cream and jam.

4. In another bowl, stir together the flour, baking powder, baking soda, cinnamon, nutmeg, and cloves. Add to the creamed mixture, stirring until the dry ingredients are incorporated.
5. Turn the batter out into the prepared pan. Bake the cake for 50 minutes or until a toothpick inserted in the center comes out clean. Transfer the pan to a rack to cool.

*Preparation time: 20 minutes*
*Yield: 8 to 10 servings*

# Mincemeat Spice Cake

If you own a food processor or electric mixer, it's really a snap to prepare this cake. Just the little box of mincemeat lends a wonderful fruity flavor and aroma to a large, satisfying spice cake. (If you don't own a food processor, you will need to chop the mincemeat finely by hand.)

| | |
|---|---|
| 2 | sticks (1 cup) butter or margarine, softened |
| 1 | cup brown sugar, preferably dark |
| 1 | egg |
| 1 | cup milk |
| 1 | teaspoon vanilla |
| 1 | 9-ounce box condensed mincemeat, coarsely broken up |
| 2 | cups flour |
| 1 | teaspoon baking powder |
| 1 | teaspoon baking soda |
| ½ | teaspoon cinnamon |
| ¼ | teaspoon nutmeg |
| ¼ | teaspoon salt |

1. Preheat the oven to 350°F.
2. Grease and flour a 9" x 13" baking pan.
3. Place the butter or margarine and the brown sugar in the bowl of a food processor, and process until the sugar is fully incorporated. Add the egg, and process until mixed in. Add the milk and vanilla, and process again. Add

the mincemeat, and process until fully mixed in. (Or you may prepare the cake using a mixer. In a bowl, cream the butter or margarine with the brown sugar until the sugar is fully incorporated. Beat in the egg, then the milk, vanilla, and mincemeat.)

4. In a large bowl, stir together the flour, baking powder, baking soda, cinnamon, nutmeg, and salt. Add to the mincemeat mixture, stirring until the dry ingredients are incorporated.

5. Turn the batter out into the prepared pan. Bake the cake for 30 minutes or until a toothpick inserted in the center comes out clean. Transfer the pan to a rack to cool.

*Preparation time: 15 minutes with
a food processor or 25 minutes
with a mixer*
*Yield: 16 servings*

# Gingered-Vodka Cake

Of all the cakes in the original *Good Cake Book*, this most special and attractive tube cake is perhaps my favorite. I bake it whenever I have left-over egg whites from another recipe. The pecans add a wonderful flavor and the taste of vodka permeates all.

*Note:* Leftover egg whites keep well for months in the freezer. I store them in a plastic container and keep track of the number of egg whites in it as I add to it. When I have enough whites to prepare this cake, I defrost the container of whites.

|   |   |
|---|---|
| 2 | sticks (1 cup) butter or margarine, softened (try to use at least half butter) |
| 1¾ | cups sugar |
| ¾ | cup (about 7) egg whites |
| ¾ | cup vodka |
| 2 | teaspoons vanilla |
| 2¾ | cups flour |
| 1 | tablespoon baking powder |
| ¾ | cup finely chopped or ground pecans |
| ½ | cup finely diced crystallized ginger |

1. Preheat the oven to 300°F.
2. Grease and flour a tube pan.
3. In a large bowl, cream the butter or margarine

with the sugar until the sugar is fully incorporated. Beat in the egg whites, then the vodka and vanilla.

4. In another bowl, stir together the flour and baking powder. Add to the creamed mixture, stirring until the dry ingredients are incorporated. Stir in the pecans and ginger.

5. Turn the batter out into the prepared pan. Bake the cake for 1½ hours or until a toothpick inserted in the highest part of the cake comes out clean. Transfer the pan to a rack to cool.

*Preparation time: 25 minutes*
*Yield: 16 to 18 servings*

# Cranberry-Orange Tea Bread

This is the classic cranberry bread, with a sweet orange batter to complement the tart berries. It's so easy to prepare that I started making it annually for Thanksgiving dinner when I was just twelve years old.

    4   tablespoons butter or margarine,
          softened
    1   cup sugar
    1   egg
    1   tablespoon grated orange rind
    ¾   cup orange juice
   1½   cups coarsely chopped cranberries
          (a blender or food processor
          works well)
    1   cup flour
    1   cup whole-wheat flour
    1   teaspoon baking soda
    ¼   teaspoon salt

1. Preheat the oven to 350°F.
2. Grease and flour a 9" x 5" loaf pan.
3. In a large bowl, cream the butter or margarine with the sugar until the sugar is fully incorporated. Beat in the egg, then the orange rind and juice. Stir in the cranberries.
4. In another bowl, stir together the flour, whole-wheat flour, baking soda, and salt. Add to the cranberry mixture, stirring until the dry ingre-

dients are incorporated.

5. Turn the batter out into the prepared pan. Bake the loaf for 1 hour or until a toothpick inserted in the center comes out clean. Transfer the pan to a rack to cool.

*Preparation time: 20 minutes*
*Yield: 8 to 10 servings*

# Spiced Pumpkin Loaf

Cocoa becomes a spice in this aromatic pumpkin loaf that's also flavored with cinnamon, ginger, and cloves. It's an ideal holiday tea bread — for gift giving or your own table.

|   |   |
|---|---|
| 6 | tablespoons butter or margarine, softened |
| 1 | cup brown sugar, preferably dark |
| 2 | eggs |
| 1 | cup canned solid-pack pumpkin (not pumpkin-pie filling) |
| ¼ | cup milk |
| 1 | cup flour |
| 1 | cup whole-wheat flour |
| 2 | teaspoons baking powder |
| 2 | teaspoons unsweetened cocoa powder, sifted if lumpy |
| 1 | teaspoon cinnamon |
| ½ | teaspoon ginger |
| ¼ | teaspoon ground cloves |
| ¼ | teaspoon baking soda |
| ¼ | teaspoon salt |
| ½ | cup coarsely chopped walnuts |

1. Preheat the oven to 350°F.
2. Grease and flour a 9" x 5" loaf pan.
3. In a large bowl, cream the butter or margarine with the brown sugar until the sugar is fully incorporated. Beat in the eggs, then the pump-

326

kin and milk.

4. In another bowl, stir together the flour, whole-wheat flour, baking powder, cocoa, cinnamon, ginger, cloves, baking soda, and salt. Add to the pumpkin mixture, stirring until the dry ingredients are incorporated. Stir in the walnuts.

5. Turn the batter out into the prepared pan. Bake the loaf for 1 hour or until a toothpick inserted in the center comes out clean. Transfer the pan to a rack to cool.

*Preparation time: 20 minutes*
*Yield: 8 to 10 servings*

# Tyrolean Nut Cake

This attractive "cake" is actually made up of 1" balls of dough that are baked side by side. Although the balls start out almost like cookies, they form a single layer when baked. To eat, use a sharp knife to cut between the edges of each original ball. Each ball-like serving is a buttery morsel, filled with crunchy walnuts.

  1  stick (½ cup) butter or margarine, softened (try to use at least half butter)
  ¾  cup plus 1 tablespoon sugar, divided usage
  2  eggs
  1  teaspoon vanilla
  1  teaspoon almond extract
2½  cups flour
  2  teaspoons baking powder
  ¼  teaspoon salt
1½  cups finely chopped walnuts

1. Preheat the oven to 350°F.
2. Grease and flour a 9" round baking pan.
3. In a large bowl, cream the butter or margarine with the ¾ cup of sugar until the sugar is fully incorporated. Beat in the eggs, then the vanilla and almond extract.
4. In another bowl, stir together the flour, baking powder, and salt. Add to the creamed mixture,

stirring until the dry ingredients are incorporated. Stir in the walnuts.

5. Break off a small piece of dough, and roll it into a ball about 1" in diameter. Place the ball in the baking pan, so it is touching the rim. Continue making balls with the dough, placing each ball next to the other so that they are just touching. The balls should be placed in the pan in concentric circles. When done, the balls will fill the entire pan.

6. Sprinkle the remaining 1 tablespoon of sugar over the top of the balls. Bake the balls for 50 minutes or until golden brown. Transfer the pan to a rack to cool.

*Preparation time: 30 minutes*
*Yield: about 36 balls, making*
*18 servings*

# One-Two-Three-Four Cake

The name of this cake doesn't refer to the speed at which it's put together. Rather, the recipe is an old one, passed along from friend to friend at a time when cookbooks weren't readily available and when people relied on memory to recall the quantities of ingredients in recipes. Thus, while a pound cake generally called for a pound of eggs, a pound of sugar, a pound of flour, and a pound of butter, this cake calls for 1 cup of butter, 2 cups of sugar, 3 cups of flour, and 4 eggs. This recipe has withstood the test of time very well, although, in the interest of lightness, a little less flour is used. Creamy White Icing (page 334) or Chocolate Butter Frosting (page 339) both go well with this cake.

2 sticks (1 cup) butter or margarine, softened (try to use at least half butter)
2 cups sugar
4 eggs
1 cup milk
1½ teaspoons vanilla
2½ cups plus 1 tablespoon flour
2 teaspoons baking powder
¼ teaspoon salt

1. Preheat the oven to 350°F.
2. Grease and flour a tube pan.

3. In a large bowl, cream the butter or margarine with the sugar until the sugar is fully incorporated. Beat in the eggs, then the milk and vanilla.
4. In another bowl, stir together the flour, baking powder, and salt. Add to the creamed mixture, stirring until the dry ingredients are incorporated.
5. Turn the batter out into the prepared pan. Bake the cake for 1 hour or until a toothpick inserted in the highest part of the cake comes out clean. Transfer the pan to a rack to cool.

*Preparation time: 20 minutes*
*Yield: 16 servings*

# CHAPTER ELEVEN

# ICINGS, FROSTINGS, FILLINGS, ETC.

## A Selection of Cake Enhancements

The cakes in this book are so flavorful that there's really no need to frost them. However, I have met people who claim they actually prefer the icing to the cake. To these people, a cake, no matter how delicious, cannot be complete unless it's adorned with a rich, creamy coating.

Icings and frostings do help protect the cake from drying out. And they also make for a festive appearance. So, for those who want their cake and icing, too, here's a selection.

- **GLAZES.** Glazes are quite thin and are usually drizzled over a cake. The top of the cake is covered with just enough glaze dripping down the sides to look appealing. Glazes are especially good on the cakes in this book because they add a hint of sweetness without overpowering the cake.
- **ICINGS.** These are a cross between glazes and frostings, being thicker than a glaze but without the heaviness of a frosting. Icings cover the cake completely and are attractively shiny.

- **FROSTINGS.** These are for the true lover of iced cakes. Thick and creamy, the frosting is applied liberally and adds a sweet, rich quality to the cake.
- **FILLINGS.** This broad term covers several different confections. Any icing or frosting can be used as a filling to sandwich two or more cake layers together. Jam is another excellent filling for cakes. Still other fillings — such as the Chocolate Cream Filling in this chapter — are made solely for this purpose and would not be suitable as an icing.
- **SAUCES.** Sauces are spooned over or around individual portions of cake as you serve them. And any sauce that's an appropriate topping for ice cream is especially terrific when a piece of cake is sitting under that ice cream.

If you are planning to ice or frost a cake, the cake must be thoroughly cooled first. Otherwise, the frosting will seal the cake, trapping the steam inside and making it soggy. Also, a warm cake will melt the frosting, turning it into a messy puddle.

# Creamy White Icing

The base for this icing is a rich white sauce, which results in a cake enhancement that's especially thick and creamy. The icing may be used as is. Or for added appeal, stir in ½ cup of chopped nuts, coconut, or semisweet chocolate morsels.

  1   **stick (½ cup) butter or margarine**
2½  **tablespoons flour**
  ½  **cup milk**
  3  **cups confectioners' sugar**
     **Pinch salt**
  ½  **teaspoon vanilla**

1. In a heavy saucepan, melt the butter or margarine. Stir in the flour, and cook, stirring, for 1 minute. Add the milk, and cook, stirring vigorously, until the mixture comes to a boil. It will be very thick.
2. Remove the pan from the heat, and beat in the confectioners' sugar, salt, and vanilla. Place the pan in a bowl of ice, and continue to beat until the icing thickens to spreading consistency.

*Preparation time: 15 minutes*
*Yield: sufficient icing for the top and sides of a tube cake*

# Chocolate–Sour Cream Icing

This is one of the easiest of all icings to prepare — and one of the richest. It's thick and glossy as well as amply flavored with chocolate.

*Note:* Cakes covered with this icing should be stored in the refrigerator.

- **6 ounces (1 cup) semisweet chocolate morsels, melted and cooled slightly**
- **½ cup sour cream, at room temperature**
- **¼ teaspoon vanilla**

In a mixing bowl, beat together all the ingredients well until the mixture is thick and glossy. Spread over the cake, letting the excess drip down the sides.

*Preparation time: 10 minutes*
*Yield: sufficient icing for the top of a 9" round or square cake*

# Caramel Icing

This is the only truly "cooked" icing recipe in the book. If you have a candy thermometer, cooked icing is simple to make; if not, it's somewhat trickier — but the results are well worth the trouble. The icing is wonderfully rich and velvety, making it an excellent complement to spice cakes, chocolate cakes, and butter cakes.

*Note:* On a candy thermometer, 240°F is the upper limit of the "soft-ball stage." If you don't have a thermometer, drop a pea-size droplet of boiling icing into a glass of cold water. You will know that the icing has been cooked sufficiently if it holds together in a ball. When you pick it up, it will flatten in your hand but not disintegrate.

> 1 **cup brown sugar, preferably dark**
> $1/3$ **cup plus 1 tablespoon milk,**
>     **divided usage**
> $2^1/_2$ **tablespoons butter or margarine**
> $1/2$ **teaspoon vanilla**

1. In a heavy saucepan, cook the brown sugar and the $1/3$ cup of milk, stirring until the sugar dissolves. Bring the mixture to a boil. Then cover, and cook over a medium heat for 3 minutes. (Do not remove the cover or stir the mixture.) Remove the cover, and let the mixture boil until it reaches 240°F.
2. Remove the pan from the heat, and beat in the

butter or margarine until the icing is thick. (An electric mixer works best.)

3. As soon as the icing has thickened to spreading consistency, stir in the vanilla and the 1 tablespoon of milk. Spread the icing on the cake immediately.

*Preparation time: 20 minutes*
*Yield: sufficient icing for the top of a*
*  9" x 13" cake*

# Lemon–Cream Cheese Icing

This is an easy-to-make, good, all-purpose icing for almost any flat cake. It goes especially well with spice cakes.

*Note:* Cakes covered with this icing should be stored in the refrigerator.

4 **ounces cream cheese, softened**
2 **tablespoons butter or margarine, softened**
1½ **teaspoons fresh lemon juice**
   **Grated rind ½ lemon**
1 **cup confectioners' sugar**

1. In a large bowl, beat all the ingredients together until thick and smooth.
2. Spread the icing over the cake.

*Preparation time: 10 minutes*
*Yield: sufficient icing for the top of a 9" square cake or a 9" x 13" cake*

# Chocolate Butter Frosting

This is one of the most popular of all frostings since it's easy to prepare and has a wonderful fudgy flavor. It is difficult to give exact proportions in this recipe — the amount of sugar you add depends on your taste. (I prefer the frosting on the bittersweet side.) The way to make this frosting, then, is to add enough confectioners' sugar to sweeten the chocolate to your liking and then to add just enough milk for the frosting to reach a good spreading consistency.

*Note:* For a layer cake, double this recipe.

> 2 **1-ounce squares unsweetened chocolate**
> 3 **tablespoons butter or margarine**
> 1 **teaspoon vanilla**
> **About 2 cups confectioners' sugar**
> **About ¼ cup milk**

1. In a medium-size saucepan, melt the chocolate with the butter or margarine. Stir in the vanilla.
2. Remove the pan from the heat, and beat in enough confectioners' sugar to sweeten the chocolate. Then beat in enough milk to achieve a good spreading consistency.
3. Spread the frosting on the cake immediately.

*Preparation time: 10 minutes*
*Yield: sufficient frosting for the top and sides of a 9" X 13" cake or a tube cake*

# Vanilla Frosting

For those who like vanilla frosting, here is a recipe that's easy to prepare. This frosting may be tinted for birthday and other celebratory cakes.

*Note:* For a layer cake, double this recipe.

> 3 **tablespoons butter or margarine, softened**
> 2 **teaspoons vanilla**
> 2 **cups confectioners' sugar**
> **About ¼ cup milk**

1. In a large bowl, cream the butter or margarine, vanilla, confectioners' sugar, and about half the milk until the sugar is fully incorporated.
2. Very slowly, beat in additional milk, about 1 tablespoon at a time, to achieve a good spreading consistency.
3. Spread the frosting on the cake immediately.

*Preparation time: 10 minutes*
*Yield: sufficient frosting for the top*
*and sides of a 9" X 13" cake or*
*a tube cake*

# Dark Chocolate Glaze

Almost fat-fee, this dark, intensely chocolate glaze takes only minutes to make and enhances any cake that goes well with chocolate.

    ¼  **cup strong black coffee**
    ½  **cup unsweetened cocoa powder**
    1  **teaspoon butter or margarine**
    ½  **cup brown sugar, preferably dark**

1. In a small saucepan, combine all the ingredients. Cook over a low heat, stirring, until the mixture is smooth.
2. Remove the pan from the heat, and let cool slightly. Pour the glaze over the cake, letting some glaze drip down the sides.

*Preparation time: 5 minutes*
*Yield: sufficient glaze for a*
    *9" X 13" cake or a tube cake*

# Chocolate Cream Filling

This filling has the texture of very rich, smooth, and creamy chocolate pudding. It's wonderful sandwiched between layers of chocolate or golden butter cake.

*Note:* Once filled, the cake should be stored in the refrigerator.

- ½ **cup sugar**
- 2 **tablespoons cornstarch**
- **Pinch salt**
- 2½ **tablespoons unsweetened cocoa powder**
- ¼ **cup hot tap water**
- 1 **cup milk**
- 1 **egg, beaten**
- 1½ **tablespoons butter or margarine**
- ½ **teaspoon vanilla**

1. In the top of a double boiler, stir together the sugar, cornstarch, salt, and cocoa. Gradually stir in the hot water until the mixture is smooth. Add the milk, egg, and butter or margarine.
2. Place the pot into the bottom of the double boiler that contains boiling water, and cook the filling, stirring, for 10 minutes or until it is thick. Remove the top of the double boiler from the heat, and stir in the vanilla.
3. Transfer the filling to a bowl, and cover with

plastic wrap to prevent a "skin" from forming on top. Chill until firm.

4. When firm, spread the filling evenly between two cake layers.

*Preparation time: 15 minutes*
*plus time for chilling*
*Yield: sufficient filling to use between*
*two 9" round layers*

# Fudge Sauce

This is an easy-to-make, incredibly rich fudge sauce that's great over ice cream and even better if there's a good-size piece of chocolate cake sitting under the ice cream. The sauce is so thick that it must be served warm, otherwise it simply won't pour. It reheats well, though, if you don't polish it off in one sitting.

*Note:* Any flavor liqueur can be used — chocolate (for those who don't want to add another taste), coffee, mint, orange, almond.

> 6 **1-ounce squares unsweetened chocolate**
> 1½ **cups sugar**
> 1 **cup light cream or half-and-half**
> 1 **stick (½ cup) butter or margarine**
> ⅛ **teaspoon salt**
> 3 **tablespoons liqueur (see *Note*, above)**

1. In a heavy saucepan, melt the chocolate over a very low heat. Add the sugar, cream or half-and-half, and butter or margarine, and heat, stirring, until the mixture reaches a sauce-like consistency, Continue cooking, over a low heat, stirring, for 5 minutes or until the sauce is very thick.
2. Remove the saucepan from the heat, and stir in the liqueur.

*Preparation time: 10 minutes*
*Yield: about 2¹/₂ cups*

# APPENDICES

## High-Altitude Adjustments for Baking*

| INGREDIENT | ALTITUDE | | |
|---|---|---|---|
| | 3,000 FEET | 5,000 FEET | 7,000 FEET |
| *Reduce baking powder* for each teaspoon, decrease | $^1/_8$ tsp. | $^1/_8$ to $^1/_4$ tsp. | $^1/_4$ tsp. |
| *Reduce sugar* for each cup, decrease | 0 to 1 tbsp. | 0 to 2 tbsp. | 1 to 3 tbsp. |
| *Increase liquid* for each cup, add | 1 to 2 tbsp. | 2 to 4 tbsp. | 3 to 4 tbsp. |

* Above 3,500 feet, you may increase the oven temperature by 25°F to set the cake faster.

# Comparative Baking-Pan Sizes

*Note:* Adjustments in baking times must be made when pan sizes are changed.

| COMMON PAN SIZE | APPROXIMATE VOLUME |
|---|---|
| **Square and rectangular pans** | |
| 8" x 8" x 1½" square | 6 cups |
| 8" x 8" x 2" square | 8 cups |
| 9" x 9" x 1½" square | 8 cups |
| 9" x 9" x 2" square | 10 cups |
| 11" x 7" x 2" rectangular | 6 cups |
| 13" x 9" x 2" rectangular | 15 cups |
| 8" x 4" x 2½" loaf | 4 cups |
| 8½" x 4½" x 2½" loaf | 6 cups |
| 9" x 5" x 3" loaf | 8 cups |

| COMMON PAN SIZE | APPROXIMATE VOLUME |
|---|---|

## Round pans

| | |
|---|---|
| 1³/₄" x ³/₄" mini-muffin cup | ¹/₈ cup |
| 2³/₄" x 1¹/₈" muffin cup | ¹/₄ cup |
| 2³/₄" x 1³/₈" muffin cup | scant ¹/₂ cup |
| 3" x 1¹/₄" giant muffin cup | ⁵/₈ cup |
| 8" x 1¹/₄" pie plate | 3 cups |
| 9" x 1¹/₂" pie plate | 4 cups |
| 9" x 2" pie plate (deep dish) | 6 cups |
| 8" x 1¹/₂" cake | 4 cups |
| 8" x 2" cake | 7 cups |
| 9" x 1¹/₂" cake | 6 cups |
| 9" x 2" cake | 8¹/₂ cups |
| 10" x 2" cake | 10³/₄ cups |
| 9" x 3" Bundt | 9 cups |
| 10" x 3¹/₂" Bundt | 12 cups |
| 8" x 3" tube | 9 cups |
| 9" x 3" tube | 10 cups |
| 10" x 4" tube | 16 cups |
| 9¹/₂" x 2¹/₂" springform | 10 cups |
| 10" x 2¹/₂" springform | 12 cups |

# Converting to Metric

| WHEN THIS IS KNOWN | MULTIPLY IT BY | TO GET |
|---|---|---|
| Teaspoons | 4.93 | Milliliters |
| Tablespoons | 14.79 | Milliliters |
| Fluid ounces | 29.57 | Milliliters |
| Cups | 236.59 | Milliliters |
| Cups | .236 | Liters |
| Pints | 473.18 | Milliliters |
| Pints | .473 | Liters |
| Quarts | 946.36 | Milliliters |
| Quarts | .946 | Liters |
| Gallons | 3.785 | Liters |
| Ounces | 28.35 | Grams |
| Pounds | .454 | Kilograms |

# Fahrenheit, Celsius, and Gasmark Equivalents

| FAHRENHEIT | CENTIGRADE | GASMARK |
|:---:|:---:|:---:|
| 250° | 130° | ½ |
| 275° | 140° | 1 |
| 300° | 150° | 2 |
| 325° | 170° | 3 |
| 350° | 180° | 4 |
| 375° | 190° | 5 |
| 400° | 200° | 6 |
| 425° | 220° | 7 |
| 450° | 230° | 8 |

# INDEX

## A

# B

baking:

# C

# F

# G

# J

# L

# M

# O

# P

# R

# T